Sabina Rachel Kałowska

NO PLACE FOR TEARS

From Jędrzejów to Denmark

Sabina Rachel Kałowska

NO PLACE FOR TEARS

From Jędrzejów to Denmark

Translated from Polish by Jerzy Michalowicz

Yad Vashem ★ Jerusalem
The International Institute for Holocaust Research

Sabina Rachel Kałowska
Uciekać, aby żyć

Academic Editor: Nahum Bogner
Language Editors: Gayle Green and Ezra Olman
Production Editor: Gayle Green

P.O.B. 3477, Jerusalem 91034, Israel
publications.marketing@yadvashem.org.il
First published in Polish by Norbertinum, 2000.

ISBN 978-965-308-418-6

Typesetting: 2w-design.com
Printed in Israel by Printiv Press, Jerusalem

Dedicated to the memory of Rafał,
And to those to whom I owe my survival.
Also to Tomasz and his family,
Who exist because I survived.

CONTENTS

Foreword 9

Chapter 1: The Early Years 11
- The Brief Joy of Childhood
- Difficulties Growing Up

Chapter 2: War 35
- The Germans Close In
- Aron Majer (Majorek)
- Rafał Kałowski
- The Ghetto

Chapter 3: On the Run 59
- Learning to Hide
- In Chlewice—At the Grzegorek's and Kita's
- At Bednarska's
- At Pawlikowa's
- At Zającowa's
- At Leszczyński's Once Again

In Dąbrówka Morska
In Słomka
In Łąkta Górna
Return to Słomka
In Opatowiec
Imprisonment and Rescue of Heniek
Together in Opatowiec

Chapter 4: Picking Up the Pieces 143
The Bitterness of Return
Anew Again
From Poland to Denmark
Returns: Poland—Israel—Denmark

Acknowledgments 191

FOREWORD

My joyous, happy childhood ended at four years old when my mother died. The shadow of sorrow from the absence of the person closest to me has remained with me ever since.

My youth was destroyed twice. The first time, I was 14 when the war broke out, tightening the noose around our lives. The second time, I was 17 and after spending a night outside the ghetto, owed solely to a turn of fortune, I learned the next morning that like all the Jews of Jędrzejów, all my loved ones had been pushed onto a train, which stopped only at Treblinka…

From that day, I started living and dying at the same time—living by running away, yet dying within. On that day, I started running for my life.

My life began many times, as if from the beginning. It often slipped through the narrow cracks between endurance and annihilation, but managed somehow to cross the abysses into which it seemed I was irrevocably sinking.

This life, which began anew so many times, lost its bright and gay colors and instead assumed pastels and shadows, the grayness of the everyday, and the blackness of despondency. And yet it refused to be snuffed out. It has endured—until today.

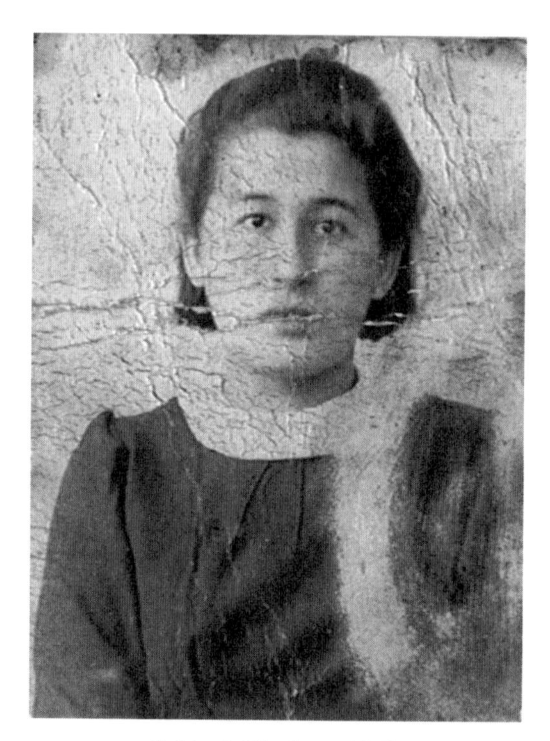

Sabina's ID photo, 1942

CHAPTER 1

THE EARLY YEARS

THE BRIEF JOY OF CHILDHOOD

I was born in Jędrzejów, where I spent my school years and the first years of the Nazi occupation. Jędrzejów boasted a long and rich history with a Cistercian monastery and the legacy of the Przypkowski family. After the January uprising in the 19th century Jędrzejów lost its municipal status, but retained its rank as a central county. Located in the Kielce district, at an important intersection, Jędrzejów remained a thriving commercial and administrative center. Already in the 19th century a railway to Kraków passed through the town and in the interwar period two narrow-gauge lines were added. The town had already joined the power grid before World War II. In 1939 Jędrzejów numbered some 14,000 residents. The Jewish population numbered 4,500.

My parents, maternal grandparents, and other relatives lived in town. I was born on May 2, 1925, in the house of my paternal grandparents, who lived outside of town. They belonged to the middle class and had a house, an orchard, a small field, and a grocery store, which sold practically everything. My grandfather also traded in grain. There was never a shortage of food or clothing, but we rarely had any luxuries.

My maternal grandfather, Mechel Landschaft, was a native of Klementów, a small locality in the Kielce district was one of ten children—seven sisters and three brothers. One of his sisters, Hendla Fajgenblat, also lived with her family in Jędrzejów, where they owned a bakery. Another sister lived in Włoszczowa, and one brother in Słomniki.

My maternal grandmother Haja Szyfra, nee Weintraub, was also born in Jędrzejów, around 1880. She had two sisters, Fajgla and Ciejwa, and two brothers. Fajgla lived in Jędrzejów. My grandmother's brother, Itzhak Weintraub, also lived in Jędrzejów, but he died before the war, leaving behind a wife and four children—three daughters and a son. Grandmother's second brother, whose name I no longer remember, resided in Sosnowiec, where he passed away before the war. His son Mordechai survived the war, left Poland for Israel, and died in Tel Aviv in 1995.

My grandparents had four children. Their eldest was my mother Chana Pesla who was called Hanka at home. She was born in 1900 and died in 1929. The second child was Ciejwa, who was born around 1906. My grandparents' next child was Aron Majer, whom we called Majorek. He was born in 1915 or 1916 and remained single until the outbreak of the war. The youngest, Haim Szmuel, whom we called Heniek, was born in 1919.

Our close and more distant relatives were scattered throughout Polish towns and villages, from Zagłębie to Little Poland. Our relatives lived in Szczekociny, Łódź, Słomniki, Włoszczowa, Miechów, Sosnowiec (where Grandmother's brother lived), Kraków, Katowice (known then as Królewska Huta), and of course, in Jędrzejów.

My father Aron Chęciński was a native of Wodzisław. His ancestors arrived there from Chęciny, a small town south of Kielce; this might explain the origin of his surname. Earlier, my father's ancestors bore the name Goldfeder. Father's parents had six children—two daughters, Fajgla (Lea) and Miriam Rywka, and four sons, Israel, Aron (my father), Abram, and Uszer.

Three of Grandfather Chęciński's sons—Israel, Aron and Abram—lived in Jędrzejów. Later, the oldest brother, Israel, moved with his family to Sosnowiec. He was a Chassid and taught Torah. His two sons, Aron and Abram, survived the war in a German camp and later moved to Israel. Aron currently lives in Tel Aviv and Abram in Holon. Fajgla also survived the war, after which she moved to Belgium, then to Israel, and finally to the United States, where she still lives. Father's brother Abram moved from Jędrzejów to Łódź several years before the war and perished in the ghetto there together with his family. My grandparents' other daughter Miriam Rywka lived with her parents in Wodzisław and ran a store there. Uszer, the youngest of Israel's children, was a merchant before the war; he lived in Karczowice, a village in the Kielce district, where he hid during the war. He was killed by local peasants.

In his youth Father was a Hebrew teacher and had a good knowledge of Torah and Jewish law. He was hired by my grandparents to teach my mother's two younger brothers Aron Majer and Heniek. Hardly anyone knew Hebrew then, but boys in religious families had to know Hebrew and the prayers. Thus, my father was hired as a home tutor for my future uncles, became acquainted with their sister and later married her.

In Wodzisław, where my Chęciński grandparents lived, there was an old synagogue, which I later learned was built in the middle of the 18th century. Grandfather Fajwisz was a cantor in the synagogue and a *mohel*; he also led prayers. Everyone in town knew him; he was widely respected and everyone called him the "first citizen."

I traveled to Wodzisław several times with my father. My grandparents had a house on the market square. I remember that Grandmother was short and had bright red hair; Miriam Rywka used to comb my hair and dress me; and Grandfather Fajwisz was associated with the Chelmno Chassidim. My father also belonged to this group. They had their prayer house, or *shtiebel*, in Jędrzejów. I remember when I was about eight the *tzaddik* of Chelmno arrived in Jędrzejów. Crowds of Chassids flocked into the railway station to greet the famous rabbi. They rode through town in a *Droshke* with high wheels, accompanied by Jews—adults and children—filled with enthusiasm and joy.

The Jews of Jędrzejów did not live in a designated part of town; their houses were scattered throughout the locality. My grandparents' house was located outside of town entirely, beyond the monastery, in the direction of Nagłowice. Beyond their house stretched the large, quite dilapidated but still beautiful estate of the Leszczyński family, who were close friends of my grandparents. I was friendly with their daughters and I visited them quite often. The oldest daughter, Maria (Maryla or Marysia), was exactly my age. Anna (Hania), the middle daughter, was one year my junior, and the youngest was Antonina, who we called Tosia.

Mother married very young, at just 19, and she gave birth to four children. We were all given biblical names because we were a religious family and this was the tradition. My older brother was named Israel and my younger brother, born two years after me, was given three names—Alter Hil Josef. I was named Rachel, but in Poland Jewish names were usually Polonized in a strange fashion and unfortunately they sounded ugly. My name, which was twisted into Ruchla, was not to my liking. It seems that others didn't like it either because on school papers I was named Rozalia, and at home I was addressed as Rózia, even though Róża would have been more compatible with my given name.

Our fourth sibling, a boy, was born in a Kraków hospital and died immediately after birth. The pregnancy had been very difficult for my mother; she was sick almost the entire time, and on a doctor's orders she stayed bedridden at home until finally she was taken back to the hospital in Kraków. Grandmother Haja went to live with her cousins in order to visit the hospital every day, and keep watch over her daughter. Grandmother was not allowed to spend the night at the hospital, so she hired a nurse to watch over my mother during the night.

Sabina's mother's grave, Kraków.
The text reads: "Chana Chęciński of the Landschaft family, deceased August, 1929 ... In memory of all the members of the Landschaft and Chęciński families who died in Nazi extermination camps in 1942."

On the morning of August 27, 1929, when Grandmother got to the hospital, my mother was dead. Mother died very young, at just 29, and her three children became motherless. I was barely four when she died.

Mother was buried in Kraków. I remember that Grandmother was terribly dejected by her daughter's death. Many people gathered at my grandparents' house. I felt, but couldn't articulate, the sorrow and pain of losing her. They grieved and I squeezed into a corner somewhere and cried. One visitor was the mayor of Jędrzejów and many years later Aunt Miecia Leszczyńska told us that she had never seen a Polish man cry so much over the death of a Jew as he did over the death of my mother. Mother was very much liked and my grandparents were widely respected among Jędrzejów's residents. Many neighbors and their families, including many Poles, expressed their condolences and my grand-parents received words of commiseration over the death of their daughter.

Later, my mother was remembered by many people on various occasions and they said I looked very much like her. I remember my mother only from a few pictures, but I do remember a song she sang to me many times, mixing Polish and Yiddish:

Czerwona róża, lipowy kwiat.
As du est bai di mame bis du zat.
(The rose is red, a linden flower.
If you eat at your mother's, you are sated.)

I remember there was a local superstition that after sewing on a button, you had to bite off the thread, otherwise your memory would be sewn up. On one occasion when Mother sewed on a button, she bit off the thread. Although I remember it as if through a fog, it is etched in my memory that when Mother was leaving for the hospital in Kraków (until then she had been treated in Jędrzejów), everybody was crying. I was told that she had long, dark, beautiful braids and wore crescent-shaped golden earrings. These earrings were meant for me, but later, in the ghetto, everything was lost.

For the rest of Grandmother's life, she couldn't get over the death of her daughter. When I was 16, she still cried, remembering her loss. On *Yom Kippur* she prayed, "I lost such a tree, such a child, a flower."

Sometime earlier my grandparents had some trouble with their other daughter, Ciejwa. A dangerous infection developed in her leg and they traveled with her to Kraków, because the city was well known for its doctors. However, the doctors did not see any alternative except to amputate the leg, to which my family had to agree. Ciejwa was 19 then and she told her mother that if it had to be so, then they could throw her into the Vistula. Ultimately, Grandmother refused to give her consent and instead got Ciejwa discharged from the hospital and brought her back to Jędrzejów. The leg looked awful—the gangrene had advanced toward the bone. There were no antibiotics then and amputation seemed the only option in order to save her life. However, someone advised my grandparents to visit a folk doctor who lived in a village about 30 kilometers beyond Włoszczowa. A drowning man clutches at straws and my dejected grandparents went to him with Ciejwa. They spent the night with Grandfather's sister and her family, the Czałczyńskis, who lived nearby. Their son, Samuel, survived the war and now lives in Paris.

The village doctor looked at the leg and said that the young girl would be dancing within three months. He said that a paste made of honey and barley flour should be put on the sick leg. This therapy turned out to be very successful. All that remained from the gangrenous area was a little depression and an insignificant scar.

Aunt Ciejwa married soon afterwards. Her husband, Mendel Nowomiejski, hailed from the nearby locality of Nagłowice and we traveled there by horse and cart several times to visit my new uncle's family. The wedding took place in Jędrzejów and then the newlyweds left for Łódź. They lived there during the war and perished in the Łódź Ghetto or possibly in a camp—my aunt, her husband and their two children. None of them survived.

After my mother's death, we moved in with our grandparents. My elder brother Israel spent some time with my Chęciński grandparents in Wodzisław, but before long he returned to Jędrzejów. Father spent whole days in the textile store he owned. He wasn't capable of taking care of three small children—to do so he would have had to close the store and stop working. In light of this situation my grandmother, who wasn't young anymore and had a whole household of her own and the store to take care of, took us in. She and her husband cared for us with great tenderness and affection, above all because of the memory of their dear daughter and their love for us, their grandchildren.

Not long after Mother's death, Father remarried and naturally our everyday and emotional ties between him and us were loosened. My early childhood experiences must have had a great mental and emotional impact. I grew up sort of doubly orphaned, without Mother and also without Father, who became attached to his new family and his children. I sensed my mother's absence and felt a deep sorrow because of it. Owing to this sorrow, which didn't always surface in consciousness, I wasn't gay, carefree or mellow. The joys of childhood were lost in a shadow that stretched over me. I was saddened by the sight of other children, especially my girlfriends enjoying their mothers' caresses. As for my grandmother, my personality, type of beauty, and face reminded her of her prematurely dead daughter and this memory also stirred sorrow and sadness.

My grandparents were loving, dedicated, caring and sensitive, but they were not my mother or father and couldn't give me what a child needs deep in her soul: the sheer presence of a mother and father.

DIFFICULTIES GROWING UP

After my mother's death and Father remarried, he continued to live in the same house on Klasztorna Street, which ran from the monastery to the market square. Before too long other children came into the world—a daughter, Bat Tzion "Zion's daughter", whose Polish name was Basia; then twins, Yaakov and Moshe; and then Nahum. Basia, the oldest of my stepsiblings, died of typhoid during the war when she was six or seven.

I lived for some time with Father and his new family. Nothing untoward happened to me in my father's household, but I didn't feel at ease with the new family. While there I was very shy, living as if on the sidelines. My stepmother, for example, when serving food, never spoke to me. I didn't want to eat, so I just sat there quietly. Grandmother noticed my difficulties and my sorrow.

My father was more religious than my grandparents and very conservative in his habits. He wanted to bring us up Orthodox and sent my older brother, Israel, to a *yeshiva* in Kielce for a year. He also sent me to a religious school. As there was no Jewish school in Jędrzejów, I went to Beis Yaakov, a school for girls, where the pupils received instruction in Yiddish, Torah, and Jewish history. I wasn't happy at the school because there were many rules to observe, which I objected to, such as wearing clothes with long sleeves and stockings. Shortly after my grandmother took me in, I stopped attending Beis Yaakov because it was too far away and instead I attended a Polish elementary school.

Sometime in 1934 or 1935 Father sold the house and bought another, larger one, which stood next to the market square on Krzywe Koło Street. Father rented out several rooms, which were used, for example, as a butcher's shop and a blacksmith's workshop. He also rented out several apartments, which faced the courtyard at the back.

Father continued to work in his textile store. His clients, especially peasants from the surrounding villages, often bought merchandise on credit, promising to pay later with food. Father often had to go back to them to claim payment. Usually, they made partial payment in the form of agricultural products.

Thursday was market day in Jędrzejów and merchants from the neighboring towns and villages came to town, as did peasants from the surrounding villages. Trade took place at two sites—the first was the market square, its stores and stalls selling agricultural produce, industrial products, clothing, and household utensils; the second site was the fairground where livestock, grains, animal feed, and construction equipment were bought and sold.

One of our cousins had a stall selling knitted garments in the market square, other cousins owned a bakery, and Father was in charge of his textile store. Market day was filled with noise, movement, all kinds of surprises, and for me, it provided an occasion to get to know various things about life and the world.

There were Polish and Jewish stores in Jędrzejów and Poles and Jews shopped in both. Usually, when a new Polish store opened, everyone went there, abandoning the Jewish stores. When it quickly went bankrupt, people would return to us, saying, "Here you can get everything!"

In Jędrzejów we felt at home but we, the Jews, were often reminded that we were foreigners. Once, when I was four or five, some Polish child yelled to me, "Hey, Jew, you crucified Christ. Get out of here and go to Palestine. You scabby unbeliever!"

"You are a Jew," I yelled back. I didn't know what a Jew was.

All in all, my father with his new family managed, although they lived very modestly as money was always tight. I don't remember him ever giving me a dress as a present. Once he established his new family, he didn't provide much toward the upkeep of my two brothers and me. On the one hand, he truly had very limited means, but on the other, he knew that at our grandparents we were provided for. We still kept in touch with our father. Sometimes he would come over for a visit.

In the aftermath of the grave illnesses of their daughters, my grandparents owed money for hospitalization, travel, and therapy, and their financial situation deteriorated. To cope with these expenses they took out large loans, which turned out to be difficult to pay off and they had to sell a plot of land. However, despite these difficulties, Grandfather's house was always open to those in need. There were many such people before the war: beggars, the homeless, and other poor people who had a habit of making the rounds of houses asking for food and money.

Grandfather always started his day with morning prayers and only afterwards would he eat breakfast. One morning, as he was about to sit down and enjoy his breakfast, a woman entered asking for something to eat. Grandfather reacted immediately with, "Give her my breakfast."

"Why?" I asked, irritated.

"Hush, be quiet, your mother wouldn't have said a word," Grandfather replied.

"This must be given to the woman," he repeated.

Whenever someone came begging, my grandparents never let him or her go away empty-handed. Even after the war started, while they still lived in their house, Grandfather would give to the needy every week and once in the ghetto, he always helped those more in need. He often used to say, "Even if you've got nothing, you must share."

Poles especially remembered his generosity and recalled his deeds, saying, "Whenever someone was in need of something and there was nothing else and no one wanted to lend money, no one wanted to 'chalk it up,' you could always count on the Landschafts." Grandmother would put into the baskets of the poor some food items, at least for the children. Grandfather would loan money. Many remembered their kindness for a long time.

The store was primarily minded by Grandmother. It had groceries, including sweetmeats, which I always lapped up or shared with my girlfriends. One could also buy notebooks and other school equipment there, as well as cigarettes, cigarette tubes, and tobacco. Before Christmas, Grandmother would order Christmas tree ornaments and gingerbread cookies. I would take the ornaments from the store and help to dress the Christmas tree in the Leszczyński home together with their three daughters.

The store did not generate much income. When people had money, they went to a Polish store where they paid with cash. But when money was in short supply, they would come to our store and make purchases on credit. "Write it down on a card," they said. The cards were pinned to the store's wall, but the debtors seldom returned and Grandfather was irritated. "This store must be shut down," he would say time after time. He himself purchased supplies from retailers, always paying in cash. So the store's cash register was always empty.

I remember, however, that the school principal bought things in the store and his purchases were entered into a notebook, but when he received his monthly salary he immediately repaid his debt to Grandfather. Police commander Piotrowicz also paid conscientiously; he was a very decent and honest person. He used to stop by at Grandfather's like a good friend. He liked to sit with him discussing the Bible and religion, as well as politics. He would buy a bag of sunflower seeds and munch on them as they talked.

Together with Uncle Majorek, Grandfather also dealt in grain. He had a storeroom located in a small granary. Peasants would sell grain to Grandfather from their wagons and a merchant retailer by the name of Wargoń would buy it. He dealt with the grain from our region. The grain trade was not very profitable and was very demanding. Profits were scant; each bag brought in only a few groschen.

My grandparents were religious, but rather tolerant in everyday matters, unlike my father who was a Chassid. They had a large prayer room in their house, and in the corner stood a special cupboard where the Torah was kept. The faithful gathered there to pray, usually more than ten men; they were neighbors and Grandfather led the prayers.

While the men prayed in the larger room, the women remained in the smaller room. Women usually knew the prayers by memory and repeated them after the prayer leader. There was a little window between the two rooms and Grandmother kept watch on Grandfather in order to follow along with the prayers and conduct the women's prayers accordingly. Grandmother knew Hebrew, prayed from the prayer book, and led the women. After the prayers ended, sweet refreshments were usually served, for which we children waited impatiently. Grandmother served glasses of sweet wine, called *Kiddush* wine, and a baked cake—usually gingerbread or apple cake.

My father prayed elsewhere. In Jędrzejów he attended a Chassidic prayer house known as a *shtiebel.* My father led the prayers there and he was known for his beautiful, strong voice. On *Rosh Hashanah* and *Yom Kippur*, however, he would come to my grandparents' house where many Jews from Jędrzejów and the environs gathered. He also led the prayers there, singing magnificently. The prayer melodies on those holy days were considered exceptionally difficult and not every cantor could cope with them. My father sang expressively and movingly. When the congregants heard my father singing the prayers, they were moved to tears. By that time, especially during the great holy days, my brothers were already duty bound to accompany him to the services and assist him. When Father sang during the service, my brothers stood on either side of him and sang with him. Certain fragments of the prayers were repeated by the congregants. Religious rules also applied to children in various degrees. Girls were supposed to fast once they reached the age of 12, but as a young girl I didn't fast, even on *Yom Kippur*. Boys had to fast only after the *Bar Mitzvah* ceremony, which took place when they were 13.

We celebrated *Shabbat* with great pomp and in accordance with the tradition prevailing in religious homes. Grandmother would light the candles. Earlier she had prepared the food. On Friday evening, the *Shabbat* meal always included chicken soup. For lunch on Saturday she served *cholent*, a baked mixture of potatoes, beans, and meat, which was prepared on Friday and then kept in the warm stove all night. Other typical *Shabbat* dishes were fish and *kugel*, which could be prepared as a cake of sorts with fruit preserves or with noodles, raisins, and sugar. Grandmother also baked *challah*, raised butter cake, egg cake or crumb cake made without butter. The entire family would gather: grandparents, my two uncles—Aron Majer and Heniek, and the three children—my two brothers and I.

The Passover holiday was exceptional both because of its rituals and the preparations that preceded it, which began long before the holiday. There was a lot of work to be done, some of it quite arduous, but the work was done in an atmosphere of festive disorder and cheerful anticipation.

Before Passover we engaged in the cleaning of the entire house. Everything was thoroughly scrubbed so that no trace of leavened bread—*chametz*—remained. Some items were exchanged for new ones, while cooking pots and other items used year-round were thoroughly scrubbed, brushed or washed to remove the last remainder of leavened dough. I helped in those chores with great enthusiasm.

Grandmother also prepared Passover raisin wine well in advance of the festivities. She would put dark and light raisins into a special jar, pour water over them, and leave them to ferment for about two weeks. Then she poured off the liquid. The wine had a small amount of alcohol and was as sweet as syrup.

She also marinated beets for the festive red borscht soup and baked special little crumb cakes with poppy seeds and she made all kinds of dishes from eggs. During Passover we ate meat, egg, and potato dishes, but we were not allowed to eat anything made from flour or peas. Needless to say, we consumed *matzot*, which were bought in huge quantities beforehand and stored in the cupboard. All the Jewish bakeries in Jędrzejów started baking *matzot* for the Jews of the town and the environs long before Passover began.

The rigorously Orthodox Jews did not buy *matzot* baked in accordance with ordinary recipes. They made their own special *matzot*, called *matza shmura*. The grain for *shmura* could not be drenched by rain during the harvest and couldn't be overripe, and it was scrupulously examined. All the activities, from cutting the grain stalks to making the flour and baking the *matzot* had to be done by hand, under a rabbi's control, whereas "ordinary" *matzot* were made by machine.

In the morning on the last day of preparations for the *Seder* meal, we would bring down from the attic a large box in which all the festive utensils, tablecloths, and service books were kept all year long, from Passover to Passover. I waited for this moment all year, anticipating with great emotion the beginning of the special ritual preceding the festivities. All the items were carefully removed from the box, unpacked, and cleaned. I excitedly helped Grandmother in all these tasks and then together we set the festive table.

The *Seder* meal was presided over by Grandfather, who sat in an armchair at the head of the table. All of us were gathered together: Grandfather, Grandmother, my uncles—Aron Majer and Heniek—and we grandchildren—Israel, Alter Josef, and I, all wearing our festive new clothes. In front of Grandfather stood the silver cup used for drinking the traditional four cups of wine, and glasses were set before everyone else, including the children. On the table was a special *Seder* plate commemorating Egyptian enslavement and the plagues: *matza*, horseradish, parsley, and salt water. Everyone read from the *Haggadah* in turn, and at certain moments my brothers asked questions regarding why this night was so different from all other nights. Grandfather would raise the four cups in turn, and all of us, including the children, drank the *Seder* wine. Melodiously, we sang Psalms and other prayers.

Passover lasted for a week, which differed from all other weeks during the year. We ate no bread, but only *matzot*, and no one got fed up with it. During the week, my Polish girlfriends would visit me to get some *matza*, which they considered a special treat. Whole families of relatives and friends gathered at our house. The adults prayed together—men under Grandfather's leadership and women under Grandmother's—and sat down at the table and talked, whereas we children played together with great abandon. For me, this was the most joyous holiday of the year, perhaps because it was also the time when spring awakened and the world turned green.

Another holiday celebrated at my grandparents' house was *Sukkot*, or the Feast of Tabernacles. A large room (*sukkah*) assembled from planks was built outside the house, to which it adjoined the courtyard. In accordance with tradition there was no permanent roof, rather each year we made the covering from corn stalks. During *Sukkot*, which lasted eight days, people, mostly men, gathered there for prayer and meals. As usual, I helped my grandmother carry the food from the kitchen.

The interior of the *sukkah* was decorated by us children with chestnuts and corn stalks, which emitted a nice smell, as well as colored paper cutouts and chains. Blankets hung from the walls because by that time the weather was cold and it was windy. Sometimes it rained and then I would run back into the house.

In the years of my childhood and adolescence I got very close to Heniek. I never called him "Uncle," and instead, always addressed him by his first name. I even called my older uncle, Aron Majer, by his first name, usually Majer or Majorek. Heniek was like an older brother to me. In fact, he wasn't much older than I and we had many things in common. Heniek taught me to write my first letters, sometimes sitting with me patiently, sometimes swatting me on my hands. He helped me with my studies, and even taught me how to embroider. Heniek was very good with his hands—he drew, sketched, and even sculpted a little. Among other things, he made special photograph frames. Once, he made a little violin, which he played! His sketches and drawings, made on large pieces of cardboard, were kept in the attic.

Sabina's Aunt Ciejwa Nowomiejska (Landschaft)

Several years before the war, Heniek went to live with Mother's older sister, Ciejwa, in Łódź. He attended a trade school there and visited us only on holidays. He was handsome and always elegantly dressed. Ciejwa's two children, Andzia and Ben (whom we called Benio), came to my grandparents' house during vacations.

There were several elementary schools in Jędrzejów, but a new school, "No. 3," was built on our side of town, near the train station. Incidentally, it was made of timber left over from the demolition of the Radziwił mansion near Nagłowice. While it was being built, the first grade was housed in the Leszczyński mansion. I attended the temporary school together with children living in our part of town and the environs. The "old" elementary school was located in the town center. There was one high school. I attended grades two to five in the newly built school. There were more than 20 children in my class, boys and girls, including five Jewish pupils. I was in the same class as

Anna Leszczyńska, who was one year my junior, but started school one year earlier. I sat with her on the same bench throughout our elementary school years. On my way to school, I often stopped by her home to walk with her and her sister. Two women servants were always busy with them: one braided their hair while the other served breakfast, and there was always a great mess. I joked about my friends' lack of independence. Grandmother also prepared my school lunch but I always braided my hair by myself, and ironed my own ribbons and collars.

I addressed Mrs. Leszczyńska as Aunt Miecia. Whenever I came over to their house or whenever she stopped by my grandmother's, not only to make purchases in the store but also for a neighborly visit, she used to say that I was her fourth daughter. She was very kind to me, but also sometimes very demanding, like a mother. Together with Grandmother they did their best to persuade me to drink milk. Whenever I stopped by to pick up Anna and her sister Maria, their mother always asked whether I had drunk my milk and did her best to talk me into drinking half a glass. Grandmother complained to everyone about my refusal to drink milk, asking people for advice on how to convince me to drink it. Even at school I was threatened that I would not be promoted to the next grade if I continued to refuse to drink milk, but nothing helped. My body refused to accept it and only now and then would I let myself be persuaded to add a bit of milk to my coffee. (Many years later it emerged that there was a good reason for my refusal. Tests conducted for a different purpose showed that I lacked a certain enzyme for digesting milk, which explained my revulsion.)

As far as I remember, there was no distinct antisemitic atmosphere in the school. Only one incident inscribed itself on my memory. A fourth-grade teacher, Maria Pawlikowska, an old, spiteful spinster who had come from Kraków, once said, "I would give 20 zloty to the poor if only we could get rid of these Jews." Sometimes she would leave us in class after school or punish us without cause. I told this to my grandmother, stressing that the punishments were imposed not only on Jewish children, but to all students, and that there was no justification for it because we had done nothing wrong. Grandmother, who was on good terms with the school principal, went to see this teacher and told her she could see to it that she lose her job within the next 24 hours. After this incident the teacher changed her attitude a little, but in general, she was a bad person to be around. She often called the Polish children "monkeys," "paupers," etc., under any pretext. Although she felt something for me, on one occasion a Jewish girlfriend who sat next to me was looking into my notebook, and Pawlikowska yelled at her, "Where are you pushing your Jewish nose?!"

She taught us the basic subjects: Polish, mathematics, and geography. Other teachers taught music and calisthenics. Once, an inspector arrived for a visit during a geography class. He asked us to name the biggest waterfall in the world. I was the only one to stand up and say the name and height of Niagara Falls, which at the time was considered the correct answer. The teacher was very pleased and proud of me.

I wasn't very talented in subjects such as mathematics and science. However, I liked history, Polish language and literature, and poetry, especially Kochanowski, Mickiewicz, and Tuwim. I had no difficulties in memorizing texts and quickly learned to recite poems from memory. It was enough for me to read a poem once before leaving for school, and then memorize it during the walk. I spoke Polish very well, without any accent, which later helped me in my wanderings during the war years. I didn't look Aryan, as people used to say then, but my lifestyle and speech helped to blur the difference.

My grandparents allowed me to attend the school Nativity play. It was then that I got to know certain carols, which later turned out to be a blessing for me. After the show, there was usually a lottery with prizes. One day, I won a live bunny, which I brought home. Grandmother laughed at me and asked, "What shall we do with this bunny? Was there no one else to win it?"

In my grandparents house there was a radio with headphones—a rarity in those days. It belonged to Uncle Majorek who would put the headphones on his ears and listen with great delight to whatever was broadcast, especially music. He often went to bed and fell asleep with the headphones on. Majorek would sometimes put the headphones on my ears and let me listen to his radio and I would sink into the world of music and fairytales for children. Later, Grandfather bought a Telefunken radio set and it became a popular attraction, bringing adults and children to my grandparents' house to listen to radio broadcasts together. On Saturday nights, children from the neighborhood came and together we listened to fairytales, taking part in these semi-mysterious radio séances.

There was a cinema in Jędrzejów, which I went to a couple of times, thanks to the easy tolerance of my grandparents, because my father did not allow this type of entertainment.

Jędrzejów school for girls—"by the monastery,"
where Sabina attended 7th & 8th grades

For seventh and eighth grade, I moved to a girls' elementary school. The building had once housed a teachers' seminary and was located near the Cistercian monastery, which was very old and well known all over Poland. In Jędrzejów we used to refer to it as "the school by the monastery." There were 30 of us in the class.

Our wonderful head teacher, whom I remember very well, was Mr. Bogdan Wojewódzki. Everyone in Jędrzejów knew the story of his marriage. He fell in love with Mala Horowitz, who had been the most beautiful child in our town. All of us girls admired her beauty. Her parents were very rich. They had a house on Klasztorna Street and owned a lumberyard. Mala converted to Catholicism and the young couple was married in church. The whole town knew about the scandal.

At first, Mala's parents renounced the marriage and disowned their daughter, but later reconciled themselves to the situation and built a cottage for the young couple near the lumberyard. I remember the beautiful Mala coming with a stroller to the school to meet her husband. She remained beautiful and we were beside ourselves with jealousy at her beauty, which was distinctly Semitic. As a Catholic she was very religious and went to mass often.

During the war, Wojewódzki had to hide his wife. He paid for this with his health. He could not recover from a prolonged cold and immediately after the war he died of pneumonia. After the war Mala returned to Jędrzejów and remarried. Her new husband was Krzysztofik from Jędrzejów, also a Pole.

As a teacher, Bogdan Wojewódzki was wonderful; all the girls admired him and no one wanted to leave the classroom. He treated us with great warmth. He addressed us Jewish students very elegantly as "girls of the Mosaic persuasion." Half the girls in our class were of the "Mosaic persuasion."

Wojewódzki was universally liked. I remember him quite well: not too tall, not as handsome as his wife, but with great personal charm. My grandmother also liked him a lot. Whenever she went to school for parent-teacher meetings she always returned very pleased.

I had many close girlfriends. I was friends with a Polish girl, Suzanna Maludzińska. We sat at the same desk. By that time I no longer went to school with Anna Leszczyńska. She had left for Częstochowa, to live with her aunt, her father's sister, and to continue her studies there. Anna's aunt and her husband, Bujakowska, owned a pharmacy and they were quite affluent. Anna's father's brother also had a pharmacy, in Opatowiec, and I spent some time there during the war.

In June 1939, I completed seventh grade. Then came the summer vacation, and then the war. One of my school friends was Tola Grzywnowicz, whose family was very rich. Unfortunately, Tola's mother died very young—Tola was only five when she became an orphan. There were six children in the family—four boys and two girls. The eldest sister married before the war. The four brothers were Julek, Józek, Lutek, and Mietek, the youngest child. Tola was the second youngest in the family and one year my senior. She lived with her older sister for a while but it wasn't good for her, so she returned home to her father, who had since remarried. They had a large home and a large plot of land close to town. Tola's father, however, died before the war and Tola's stepmother met a tragic end—at the beginning of the war, as early as 1939, she was shot to death by the Germans. Thus, Tola's childhood ended when, at the tender age of 13, the house passed into her care, as did the care of her four brothers, even though three of them were older than her. Tola also had a stepsister, Marylka, from her father's second marriage.

Grandmother went to visit often. Tola liked my grandmother very much and often said that she replaced her mother to some extent. Grandmother helped Tola and advised her on many practical and everyday matters, as little Tola was quite helpless. Our houses were only two kilometers apart, so we visited each other quite often. We attended the same school, but it seems that we were in the same class for only one year; I think it was the third grade. For a while, Tola stayed with her sister in Chorzewa, where her husband was a forester in the Chorzewa woods. However, Tola didn't like it there and she returned to her father's home. Tola's eldest brother, Julek, lived in Warsaw before the war and because he was so citified we called him "Warsaw Man."

In Jędzejó there was one synagogue and several prayer houses, known as *shtiebelach* or *beitei medrash*, each belonging to a different stream of Judaism. There was also a left-wing organization headed by a man named Grosswasser. Those who attended the meetings were mostly young and poor. One day, while the Chassidim were praying, there was a meeting of young left-wingers taking place next door. The leader of the meeting said that that day's meeting would be directed against God.

The persecution of Jews, as it intensified in the pre-war years, affected the development of left-wing and communist views. For Jews, this was a very difficult period. As a student in elementary school I didn't experience much harassment, but in the secondary schools and universities young Jews felt the brunt of the anti-Jewish atmosphere. Limitations were imposed on the enrollment of Jewish youth in schools and acceptance to university and officer ranks in the army were practically off limits.

Father did his army service in the famous Podhalański Regiment. As he was religious he did everything he could not to eat the army rations, because the food was not kosher. For this reason he suffered digestive problems, which plagued him until he died. He very much wanted his army service to be over, because it was so unpleasant and difficult for him. Grandfather Mechel, on the other hand, served four years in the Tsar's army before World War I and he was very proud of this. Whenever he told stories about his army service, Father mocked him and Grandfather would reply, "What about you? At least I was in the music corps, in the Caspian district, under Commander Kuropatkin!"

Grandfather told us that religious tolerance prevailed in the Tsar's army. Jews, for example, went to synagogue on Saturday to pray, which was even obligatory. Grandfather was very musically talented and played the cornet in the army orchestra. For some time, he served in Persia. He returned from his army service in full uniform, as was the custom then. He kept his army fur coat made of thick, green fabric, and lined with fur, until the end. He used to taunt my father, "Once there was an army, not like today, when soldiers return home dressed in rags. At least I saw a piece of the world." In fact, in the interwar years the Polish army, in which Father served, was different; Father and many others were persecuted because of being Jewish.

Father told us the story of Isoroski, a Jewish army recruit, who was constantly knocked about. He was ordered to fall on the ground and get up, and then told to get under the table and say over and over, "I am a dog, Isoroski the Dog." Once, Father was ordered to jump onto a horse and when he failed again and again, because he didn't know how to do it, the corporal harassed him. Other Jewish recruits received the same treatment. On the other hand, the course of Uncle Aron Majer's army service was quite exceptional. He only attained the rank of corporal, but he was an exemplary soldier and liked by everyone. Uncle Majorek thought of himself as a true-blue soldier. Whenever he got a pass and came to visit us we would recognize him from a distance. He always made a show with his sword and used it to knock on the door. "Well, it looks like Majorek has arrived," someone would say. He liked the army and often got passes home for good behavior. He would usually visit on Saturdays or other holy days. Majorek was discharged from the army shortly before the war began and after he returned home he took up grain trading.

I remember that he had two horses and both were gray with black and white stripes, as if they were twins. He adored them and rode, cleaned, and generally looked after them. On one occasion one of the horses jumped over me, but did not touch me, otherwise I would have met a sorry end.

My grandparents employed a boy named Janek Madej. He was motherless and his father was very poor and worked tending other people's cows. Janek took care of our horses and rode a large commercial wagon hitched to four horses. He rode to a retail point in the city of Będzin, in the Zagłębie region, run by a man named Gabin, where he sold our flour and eggs and brought back coal, which was bought by our neighbors.

For a period of time, Grandfather and Father worked as partners. They hired two assistants and had two freight wagons, each hitched to two horses. The second assistant was Tadek Madej, Janek's cousin. Tadek's mother used to come to Grandmother to help her with household chores and in the garden. Janek and Tadek rode in convoy to Zagłębie. The route was long and dangerous, because parts of it crossed woods, and more than once the wagon drivers were assaulted by bandits.

There were also humorous situations. On one occasion, the eggs, which Janek transported in a box, broke and after he arrived in Będzin, Janek asked Gabin to make him scrambled eggs from 30 broken eggs!

Janek was very attached to my grandparents, who treated him as one of their own, almost like a family member. While he still worked for them he was conscripted and he came to visit us whenever he got a pass. When he received vacation for Christmas he also came to my grandparents, where he felt at home, rather than going to the Polish neighbors he knew. Grandmother made a traditional Christmas dinner just for him—red borscht, sauerkraut with peas and mushrooms, and macaroni with poppy seeds. Janek was deeply moved by Grandmother's generosity and loving care.

I also liked Janek a lot. I taught him to write and he told me all kinds of made-up stories, for which he had great talent. He always promised to bring me back some souvenir or sweetmeats from his journeys and meanwhile he encouraged me to bring candy from Grandmother's store. Of course I did so, out of a desire to listen to more stories. Janek Madej passed away shortly before the war.

Uncle Majorek also traveled many times to Zagłębie, especially to Będzin, where he settled the accounts with Gabin the merchant. He got to know Gabin's son, a young man his age, and they became friends. Once, young Gabin came to visit us and Majorek decided to introduce him to Miss Todzia Górski, a pretty and affluent landowner from Kraków, which isn't far from Jędrzejów. The two young men traveled to Kraków on a horse-drawn narrow cart, which they borrowed from the Leszczyńskis. Young Gabin, a handsome man, was dressed in his officer's uniform. Before he climbed onto the wagon, he noticed that his shoes were not shiny enough and he returned home to polish them to perfection. Grandmother, who witnessed this episode, said, "Well, young man, nothing will come of it." She believed that one must not turn back before setting out on a journey. And she was right. The suitor traveled to visit his belle for two years, bringing her expensive presents, including a piano and radio. However, it was all in vain as, eventually, Miss Górska said she would not marry a merchant and the marriage never took place.

Two or three years before the war, Grandfather Mechel got involved in a complicated litigation concerning forest rights. In 1936 or 1937, 40 Polish farmers, including Grandfather, bought forests and fields in Chorzewo, which were owned by a wealthy Jew named Wilczek who lived in Łodź but often came to the Jędrzejów region, because his two cousins lived on an estate nearby.

For reasons that remain obscure, Wilczek invalidated the deed of sale even though it had been properly drawn up and formulated in accordance with the law. The buyers sued Wilczek in a Kielce court and gave my grandfather power of attorney to appear in court on their behalf. This was testimony to the great respect they accorded him.

Preparations for the investigation lasted a long time. Grandfather traveled to Kielce many times, driven by his desire to attain justice. Wilczek was very busy and exerted all kinds of pressure on the court to delay the start of the trial, whereas, in fact, he wanted to stop it from taking place.

Grandfather was very worried about this matter and kept in touch with the lawyers. He kept saying that justice had to be attained. The interested parties gathered at his home, trying to make plans for the next move. They trusted Grandfather fully, and even called him "Lawyer."

Heniek, who lived in Łodź at the time, and was also somehow involved in the litigation, once heard Wilczek say, "If your father is so smart that he defends everyone, then he'll get what the others get. If he could talk to me face-to-face then his investment would be returned to him." But Grandfather never agreed to this compromise and maintained solidarity with the other Polish farmers. In any event, nothing was resolved before the outbreak of the war.

In the years leading up to the war, antisemitic attitudes were displayed with growing frequency and visibility. The Kielce region was known for its antisemitic incidents and for us it was very unpleasant. There were antisemitic organizations and youth groups that targeted Jewish stores. In Jędrzejów the leader of the National Democracy Party (*Endecja*) was a man named Siewior, who lived on Klasztorna Street. Thursday was market day in Jędrzejów and many farmers from the area came to town. On these days the nationalists prevented people from buying at the Jewish stores, broke store windows, and engaged in other provocations. On one occasion, they also attacked my grandfather on his way home, causing a head injury. Another time, they attacked my father's house on Klasztorna Street, pelting it with stones.

There were many arson attacks on Jewish homes in the years 1937–1938. Among others, they set fire to the Weintraubs' house. They were related to Grandmother and lived nearby. Their house burned to the ground and as they had no means to make the necessary repairs the family had to leave the smoldering ruins and rent an apartment from a family living nearby.

Two attempts were made after dark to set fire to Grandfather's farmstead, succeeding to burn it to the ground on the second attempt. Neighbors rushed to help and we doused the flames with water. A fire engine arrived soon after. We were then paralyzed by the strength of the elements and shocked by the human hatred. Unfortunately, Grandfather did not have time to rebuild the farmhouse. However, thankfully the main house was spared.

In the same area the house of the poor Borensztajn family, who dealt in milk, was set on fire. Only part of their house was salvaged and thereafter the Borensztajns moved into the only remaining room. They later added an entrance hall. Later, provocateurs set fire to the house of Borensztajn's brother and part of his house burned down. Somehow they cobbled together a new wall and continued living there in the smaller house. Their barn and its contents burned to the ground.

The antisemitic mood and actions reached their crescendo with the death of a teacher I knew. Three years before the war my grandparents had hired a private tutor to teach me and several other Jewish girls the Jewish prayers, Torah, and just enough Hebrew for us to read the prayer books. He came from Staszów twice a week and held classes in the houses of each member of the group, receiving payment from each family. He was slightly handicapped, with one paralyzed hand. We didn't like him because he was very demanding, sometimes threatening us with a stick, and even hitting us.

This man became the victim of a terrible tragedy, which seemed to top the antisemitic events in the Kielce region. In Staszów, bandits entered the home of a Jewish family with several children. My teacher was there, conducting a class for the children. The attackers murdered the entire family, and the teacher, who tried to escape, met the same fate.

The news quickly spread throughout the entire region, provoking our fear and sense of endangerment. After this terrible murder—whose perpetrators were never found—and following a series of arson incidents in our area, I began to be scared, particularly in the evening, and that fear never left me—it was as if it became a part of me—but I didn't say a word to anyone because I was ashamed. Even today I cannot forget this fear, which would grip me when I went to bed, especially before falling asleep or at dawn when

I woke up earlier than the others. "Good Lord," I thought, "if they attack us where could I hide, would I be able to escape?" Right-wing organizations and fascist storm troopers continued to carry out their campaign of intimidation, so that the Jews would not have a moment of peace.

In the summer of 1939, when I was 14, my stepmother became seriously ill. She had pulmonary problems and Father sent her to Szczawnica to recuperate. Father asked me to help with caring for my younger siblings and I looked after them for two or three weeks during the last month of vacation before the war began. Taking care of the children was my only duty, as a hired woman came to help with the cleaning and cooking. Father was busy with his store all day long. Grandmother would come to help and give me advice. The twins—Moshe and Yaakov—were so alike that Grandmother could never tell them apart. She always had to ask who was who. Both had blue eyes just like their father, whereas their hair was blond like that of their mother. Towards the end of the summer, I returned to my grandparents and when the war broke out I was living with them, together with my uncle Aron Majer and my brothers.

CHAPTER 2

WAR

THE GERMANS CLOSE IN

We heard the news about the outbreak of war on the radio. Shortly after, refugees from Zagłębie, Upper Silesia, and Sosnowiec, on the run because the Germans had already entered those regions, started passing through Jędrzejów. Convoys of wagons and people on foot passed through, with some staying the night. Many families found lodgings for the night at my grandparents' house. They made a brief stopover and then continued eastward.

When the Germans got closer to Jędrzejów, we stayed put as there was nowhere to escape to. In any event, no one knew how things would turn out. However, just before the Germans entered our town, people fled. They were gripped by fear, hearing gunfire and bomb explosions. This was the time to escape. Beyond Jędrzejów stretched the Chorzewo Forest and we set out in that direction. Grandmother loaded our essentials, including some food, onto a pushcart. We left the house just before the Germans arrived.

To the sound of bombs exploding, we managed to reach the woods. The fear of a child after an explosion is inexplicable! I was terrified. I hid under the cart and nestled in as deep as I could. There was nothing to drink in the woods, but because some farmers had escaped with their cows, we were able to acquire some milk. I managed to temporarily overcome my aversion to milk just so as to be able to drink something.

While we were fleeing into the forest, my younger brother Alter Josef was at our father's house. In the disorder that reigned, he left Father's house and set out for our grandparents' house, which lay at the edge of town. He managed to reach the house, but found it empty. There was no one else around, because the neighbors had also fled, leaving behind their empty houses. Disoriented and frightened—he was only 12 at the time—Alter decided to return to Father's house. Returning alone, he encountered some Germans who were heading in convoy to the market square. They caused him no harm and even gave him a ride in their wagon. Later, Alter told us he had cried, frightened as he was by the whole situation, telling the Germans he was a Jew, begging them not to kill him, not to shoot him to death. He couldn't explain why he had behaved like this. In any event, the Nazis didn't lay a finger on him and in this fashion he "entered" Jędrzejów, together with the Germans, and later reached Father's house.

We, on the other hand, spent that night and the following day in the forest. Everyone wanted to know what the situation was, what had happened to their homes and properties. The German army continued forward on the main road, passing near to where we were. They avoided the byroads, which remained empty. I shivered with fear at the sound of the bombers' characteristic buzz. When the bombs fell and their explosions could be heard, I was relieved, knowing that this time we had been spared, but the expectation of the next bombardment was the worst. These first war experiences, filled with fear, have etched themselves deeply in my memory.

Grandmother had once told me about the First World War, about the soldiers shooting with machine guns, and I could only imagine how the people went into hiding in their basements. But my first personal encounter with war was much worse.

Eventually, several men came out of the forest and set out for town to determine the situation there. Grandfather, who was very courageous because of his service in the Tsar's army, of which he was very proud, also set out with the others. The Germans, however, noticed them immediately and started shooting. The group of men threw themselves on the ground and crawled back into the forest. One person, a Pole named Król, was killed.

The Germans were everywhere. However, they weren't attacking the civilian population so staying in hiding made no sense anymore. Besides, everyone wanted to get home, despite their fears. All those who were hiding in the forest—Poles and Jews from Jędrzejów and the surrounding villages—started trooping toward their homes. Grandfather remembered the Germans from the First World War and he had preserved his positive impressions. Upon returning to Jędrzejów he saw a German Wehrmacht soldier and reached out to shake his hand.

The refugees from Zagłębie, however, kept on moving until tragedy struck. In Opatów a bridge was loaded with a convoy of carts and columns of refugees when, all of a sudden, the Germans started bombarding the bridge. A terrible massacre took place and many people, as well as horses and cattle, perished.

When we returned, we discovered the house and the store had been looted and practically nothing remained. German soldiers had killed all the fowl; only their feathers remained in the courtyard and the house. The same thing had happened everywhere: The Germans looted everything—food and property—and hurried along.

After his return home, Grandfather did not open his store. Almost everything had been looted and it was impossible for him to return to his previous occupation. There was nothing left.

After a while, my grandparents' youngest son, Heniek, arrived. It had taken him a week to travel from Łódź by bicycle and on foot in order to find out whether we were alive and to stay in his parents' house. He was completely exhausted from the long, difficult, and dangerous journey. He brought us the first piece of news about Aunt Ciejwa and her family, as until then we had no idea what had happened to them.

Heniek stayed with us and was very resourceful. He started trading, because somehow a living had to be made. He got in touch with a miller and sold flour on the black market. Milling for oneself was forbidden, but this miller did it on the sly, and then Heniek sold the flour.

At that time, Grandmother baked bread once a week. We milled the grain in secret using milling stones, which were hidden immediately after being used. At the beginning of the war almost every family baked its own bread from our "milling flour." This went on until 1941. My grandparents often handed out bread to the poor even if there was not enough for us. However, someone must have informed the Germans about this "business," because one day they arrived at our house and started searching the house, making a huge racket. They told me to move from one spot to another. During the search they saw the Torah. "*Ach, Donnerwetter*," one of them cursed, "*ein Rabiner?*" They were looking for Heniek, but someone had given him and the miller advance warning and they had managed to escape in the nick of time to Rakoszyn. Grandfather was very sick and was in bed with a high fever, but the Germans paid no heed and removed the sick man forcibly from his bed and took him with them. Thankfully, due to Grandmother's strenuous efforts he only spent several hours under arrest and was then released.

A Jew named Tajtelbaum, who had some shady contacts and dealings with the Germans, arranged with the Germans the release of prisoners, of course for money and, following Grandmother's efforts, it was he who helped Grandfather. Tajtelbaum met a tragic end. He had been involved in mediating the release of prisoners for a long time. One day some Germans from Kielce came to his house and began tormenting his whole family. They did not kill them right then and there, but kept tormenting them like animals, drinking alcohol and throwing bottles at the poor family. In the end, people said the Tajtelbaums died a horrible death.

In the winters of 1939 and 1940 the Germans recruited men to work shoveling snow. They also told the men to shave their beards—Grandfather had a pretty, thick and trimmed beard, whereas Father's was much longer, and they instructed the Jews to wear armbands—white with a blue six-point star sewn onto it. The children, too, were required to wear the armband. Whenever it was necessary and possible we would take them off to avoid being recognized, especially when we were carrying food.

At first, everyone lived in his or her own house. It was still possible to move around relatively freely and life retained a semblance of normality. In the winter of 1940 I even went with my father to a Jewish wedding in Chorzewo, which was not far away. My girlfriend, Zuzia Maludzińska, lent me a dress and we traveled there by sledge. The groom, whom I already mentioned, was the manager of the Wilczek estate. There was no rabbi and Father was invited to conduct the ceremony. Apart from Jews, many Poles also attended the wedding, and after seeing my father presiding over the ceremony the young boys who asked me to dance referred to me as a "priest's daughter."

During the war I spent some time with my paternal grandparents in Wodzisław. We traveled there in 1940, shortly before Passover, and I carried the special flour for baking the *matza shmura*. We traveled on a horse-driven cart belonging to the Krzysztofiks, a Polish family who befriended my grandparents as they had a daughter and a son-in-law in Wodzisław; his name was Głodzik and he worked as a clerk.

Back in Jędrzejów, Father fell on hard times and was finding it more and more difficult to live in the town center. In the spring of 1941, Father and his family moved to my grandparents'. My grandparents, who were always very kind, gave him a separate room with a kitchen. Father left his house unattended and soon after some Polish families moved in.

In this fashion all of us lived together and although there was considerable congestion, my grandparents had made a decision. It was very noble of them and everyone admired them for it. After all, their daughter, my mother, was no longer among the living, while Father had established a new family and they had no obligations towards him, especially since they were the ones raising his first three children. But they pitied him, seeing how difficult his situation was. In any event, Grandfather respected my father very much. Grandmother also cared very much for us children and she retained this attitude in the difficult years of occupation.

The Germans opened just one school—an agricultural school for boys— where only agricultural subjects were taught, as well as a bit of mathematics. This school was located in Skroniów, on the other side of Jędrzejów. Several secret study groups were established in Jędrzejów and I attended one of those. The meetings took place in a different house each time, but often took place at the Leszczyński's house as it was safest there. Hania and Maryla Leszczyński, whom I befriended, also took part in these clandestine study groups. The meetings sometimes took place in our house, with my grandparents' knowledge and permission.

These study groups began in the winter of 1940 and I attended the meetings almost throughout that year, completing one grade. Several people conducted the study groups, including Mr. Żurek, a lawyer who, like many others, had been uprooted from his home in Greater Poland (Wielkopolska) when the Germans incorporated it into the Reich, and ended up in Jędrzejów.[1] There were also teachers from the Jędrzejów high school, as well as Mr. Artymiak, a school principal from before the war, who was only present during exam time.

Thanks to these study groups, Maryla Leszczyńska completed her matriculation exams and immediately after the war was admitted to medical school. During my participation the following people also attended: Maryla and Hania Leszczyński; Kazia Pluta (or Plucianka, as she was called); Genia Hańbówna, an only child; Danusia Widurska, who must have been slightly older than us because she had attended high school before the war; Danusia's younger brother; Zuzanna Maludzińska, Roman's daughter; and Kazik Legomski, Zuzanna's first cousin. We were nine students altogether, including me, the only Jew. These secret study groups continued until the end of the war, but I had to stop attending after we got expelled to the ghetto. However, I did accidentally overhear one more lesson in 1943 when hiding in the Leszczyński's.

Staszek, the only son of the former high school principal Artymiak, began courting Maryla Leszczyńska. She was only 17 when their courtship began in 1941. An engagement ceremony took place, but ultimately, Maryla broke off the engagement and the wedding did not take place, even though she was very much liked by her future mother-in-law and Maryla's father supported their relationship.

Despite the limitations and bans during the occupation, Heniek was very active in maintaining contact with many people, trading whatever he could, and helping my grandparents to survive. He often visited the Krzysztofik family, who were friendly with my grandparents. He played cards with their son, Stasiek, who was a judge. Whenever it was nearing the time for Friday evening prayers and Heniek had not yet returned home, Grandmother sent me to fetch him, because Grandfather got very upset if he was not home on time. On other days, when it was already late and he had not yet shown up, Grandfather would lock the door, telling us not to let Heniek in. Grandmother would then ask me to keep watch and open the door for Heniek when he came back. I did this willingly because I took pity on him.

1 At the beginning of World War II, nearly a quarter of the pre-war Polish areas were annexed by Nazi Germany and placed directly under German civil administration. An estimated 780,000 Poles were expelled.

ARON MAJER (MAJOREK)

Before the war, Majorek had done his army service in Kielce and later moved to the reserves. While serving in the artillery corps, he told us many stories about the guns. He was very much liked in the army and was decorated, which was very rare for a Jew. Majorek was a very dashing soldier and once, when he received a Saturday pass, he came to town with his superior officer. They arrived on horseback and before entering they made a big show with their swords.

Majorek had a thick army songbook, which he brought home with him. I liked to leaf through it and sing the words to either the melodies that I knew or I simply composed my own melody. I would often sit for a long time humming these army songs. I still remember some of the lyrics today.

Majorek was called up and left home early in September, never to return. Now and then we got some news about him. One cousin, Josef Białokamiński, who died in Israel several years ago, returned to Poland after years of wandering in the East, and told us that he had met Majorek once. He was one of the few people we knew who had seen Majorek and could tell us something about him.

In September 1939, when the Polish army units were heading east, they were already dispersing and in their continuing flight they clashed with the Soviet offensive. It was said that Polish soldiers were discarding their uniforms, trying to survive any way they could. According to Cousin Josef, Majorek was arrested by accident when he was riding a bus. Something fell from his hands and one of the Russian women on the bus informed the authorities that Majorek was trading on the black market, which carried a severe penalty. Majorek was arrested and while in jail he went on a hunger strike and refused to accept food for five days, claiming he had been unjustly accused. When our Cousin Białokamiński met him, apparently he was starving and Josef gave him a sausage, which he gobbled up. Later, Majorek and Josef went their separate ways and nobody knew what happened to him after that.

Josef Białokamiński also spent five years in various prisons, being moved from one to another. However, it appears that thanks to his prison stints he was spared the Holocaust. After the war he returned to Poland, found me, and told me what he knew about Uncle Aron Majer.

We once received news about Majorek from his friend, Krzysztofik, a native of Jędrzejów. Krzysztofik was arrested by the Russians and put in jail in Lutsk or Rovno. After he managed to get out and return home, he told us about his meeting with Majorek. Krzysztofik later moved to Rovno in Volhynia and became a judge. Although he had seen my uncle, he didn't know anything about his later vicissitudes.

In the first stages of the war, in 1941, my grandparents tried to get Majorek released from the army, but after the outbreak of the German–Russian war in mid-1941, such attempts could succeed only through the mediation of the German authorities. My grandparents' efforts to locate him may have, in fact, harmed his cause, as we learned that when the Soviets read out the names of the people whose families were searching for them and someone responded, instead of handing him over to the Germans, he was immediately sent into the Russian interior, with a sentence of five years of exile. Only after the war did I learn that my uncle had been exiled to the city of Gorki. We don't know anything more about Uncle Aron Majer—where or when he died, or where he was buried.

I liked Aron Majer very much. After my mother's death I became very close to her two brothers, whom I treated like my older brothers as the age difference between us was only six and ten years. Because of this small age difference, I felt no need to address them in any overtly respectful way. Aron Majer was the older brother and was very well respected and liked by everyone who knew him. After the war people constantly asked me where he was and if he had survived. They couldn't forget him. He was kind to everyone and was always willing to help. If someone asked him to lend them some money, he would immediately reach into his pocket and hand over the money. He was often asked to help with this or that and he was always available.

This was also the case during the war. The Leszczyńskis' cousin from Kraków ended up somewhere in Volhynia, escaping like many Poles to the east ahead of the Germans. Uncle Majer had met them there, taken them under his care, and gotten hold of some food for them. Another person who met my uncle was an acquaintance from Jędrzejów, chairman of the "Społem" cooperative, who returned to our town in November, having escaped earlier. He went to my grandparents and told them that he had met Majorek and Majorek had helped him, and now he wanted to reciprocate the favor. It seems that he arranged an allocation of coal for my grandparents.

Before the war, Uncle Aron Majer had a bicycle. Once, I took it to teach my friend Zuzanna Maludzińska how to ride it. During one of her attempts she crashed against the curb and fell off the bike, which emerged all twisted from the accident. I brought the bicycle home and when Majorek saw it, he asked, "Who did this?" I replied that I had done it. True to his nature, he didn't punish me.

When I lived with my father for a while, my grandmother visited us from time to time and noticed that I wasn't looking very well; I missed my grandparents' house terribly. Grandmother must have told the story back home, because shortly afterwards Uncle Aron Majer came to my father's house and said with a tone that brooked no resistance, "Grab your books and your school bag. You are coming to live with us." All my memories of him retain the warmth and closeness I felt for him.

Majorek was single but had been engaged to an affluent girl from Rakoszyn. I went there on one occasion, but my memories of this visit are vague. For her part, she visited my grandparents several times, also during the war, when we no longer knew Majorek's whereabouts, to try to get some news about her fiancé. My grandparents liked and respected her.

Unfortunately, she met a tragic fate. Her village was some 25 kilometers from Jędrzejów. During the war she went into hiding together with another girl, in anticipation of traveling to Germany. They already had Aryan papers, little crosses, and baptism certificates. They stayed near Nagłowice, not far from where I was hiding, in Chlewice. As they hid in some small room awaiting an opportunity to leave, a peasant denounced them to the Blue (Polish) Police, who in turn notified the Germans of their discovery of two young Jewish women. The Germans came and took both of them. By that time there was no longer a ghetto in Jędrzejów to which they could have been sent and single persons or small groups were not shipped to concentration camps. Usually, the apprehended Jews were shot right then and there, immediately after their capture or arrest.

The two girls were shot to death in a forest, en route from Chlewice to Jędrzejów. I was shown the spot when I passed through on my way to another hiding place. The horse-drawn cart driver who transported them to their execution said later that they had given him a piece of fabric, telling him, "Take this as a souvenir for taking us to our deaths."

I learned about this ignominious event while in Chlewice. The incident became well known and people talked about it for a long time. This took place at the end of 1942. The peasant who informed on them perhaps, like many others, thought they had something valuable with them and that he would get rich in this fashion. I don't know whether they were betrayed by the person who kept them in the small room or by someone else.

RAFAŁ KAŁOWSKI

Like many new arrivals, Rafał Kałowski showed up in our area because he had been uprooted by the Germans from his home in Grodziec, in Konin County. Since he was a teacher by occupation and had been an elementary school principal before the war, he was referred to work in the agricultural school in Skroniów, a town not far from Jędrzejów. He settled there and served as the school's principal. However, later, in the spring of 1941, he moved to Jędrzejów.

He always regarded the Jews with great fondness and told the mayor of Jędrzejów that he wanted to live with a Jewish family. They deliberated for a while over where would be the best place to put him up and finally came up with the Landschaft's. Rafał came to us, took a look at the house, said he liked it very much and that he wanted to live in one of the rooms. It was then that

Rafał Kałowski, c. 1937

he met me for the first time. Laughing, he told me the story of how, before the war, he had held secret meetings with a rabbi's daughter without her parents' knowledge.

Rafał descended from aristocracy with the coat of arms of Korab, a family hailing from Łęczyca, a small town in Greater Poland. His family owned a huge mansion with about 20 hectares of land and orchards in Rychwał. The family mausoleum, where his parents were buried, was situated there. He had two brothers and a sister.

Rafał's older brother, Adam, worked for 20 years as a musician in America, giving private music lessons. It was also in America that he met and later collaborated with Feliks Nowowiejski, the composer of the song "*Rota*". Adam returned to Poland and lived in Poznań where he bought a tenement, which was managed by an administrator, because some of the apartments were rented out. Together with his wife and three children, he then moved to Rabka because its mineral waters were beneficial to the health of children. They bought a large lot, aiming to build a house on it. It was there, in Rabka, that the war surprised them.

Rafał's other brother, Ludwig, had also immigrated to America and he passed away there. Rafał's sister, Marta, also went to America as a young 16-year-old, where she was invited by her childless aunt. She got married there, but died as a young woman, before the war. She had three children, but two of them died. Rafał kept in touch by letter with the only surviving child, Żenia.

Following his graduation from high school, Rafał was called up to the Tsar's army and completed the officer's course. During the First World War he fought as a Russian army officer on the northern front, in the area of Saint Petersburg and in Finland. He also took part in the Polish–Bolshevik War in 1920. Later, he was moved to the army reserves and started working in a school, leaving his sword and uniform at home.

Rafał had his own apartment and made a good salary as school principal, about 400 zloty per month. This was a large amount, as the average salary before the war was only about 100 zloty. So with a salary four times the average, he could live quite well.

Rafał was a motorcycle freak. Before the war he rode a BMW—modern, solid, large, and very expensive. Such a motorcycle cost 2,000 zloty but because he lived alone he could accumulate savings; he had 15,000 zloty in the bank. However, when the war broke out he lost everything. When he was called up, he mounted his motorcycle and rode to the mobilization point. He took part in the September Campaign, sharing the dramatic vicissitudes of the Polish army. German bombardment came from every direction and his unit kept retreating eastward, first to the line of the Vistula, and then further east, toward the Bug River.

After his unit was finally smashed, Rafał and a group of other Polish officers wanted to break through to the west. As they advanced, still on the eastern side of the Bug River, they ran into a Red Army unit, which captured them and put them in prison. They were taken to some little town and put in a crowded cell, under terrible conditions. After a while all of them were called outside to a large pit, which had been dug nearby. They all thought they were going to be shot on the spot and thrown into the pit, but this did not come to pass. The Russians carried out a selection, which would be the first of many. They checked the prisoners' identity papers and sentences were passed according to each prisoner's civilian occupation. Rafał was told to cross over to the other side, not to be released, but to be transferred to another camp. Several of his acquaintances—Kobyliński and Górski among others—were later shot to death in Katyń.

Rafał ended up in a freight car heading east. At some point he noticed that another freight train was traveling in the opposite direction, west toward Poland. Both trains were moving quite slowly and Rafał took advantage of the opportunity and jumped from his train to the other one. The guards tried to shoot him, but missed. Nobody stopped the trains and he managed to escape. Sometime later he jumped off this "salvation train," discarded his uniform, and started walking. He was famished and ate wild turnips. Finally, he reached some village or other and managed to lay his hands on some civilian clothes.

Rafał started trekking toward the Poznań region, his native area. He traveled almost exclusively by foot, without letting his guard down, and again survived on raw turnips he found in fields along the way.

Finally, in November, he managed to reach Rychwał, his hometown. In his absence, a rumor had spread that he had perished. Everyone was overjoyed at his return. Meanwhile, Rafał's aunt, his mother's sister, had died. She was laid to rest in the family mausoleum.

Rafał did not stay long in Rychwał, but returned to Grodziec, about ten kilometers away. He took up residence in the official apartment that had been assigned to him as school principal. However, he could not resume his

Rafał Kałowski in the Russian Imperial Army, c. 1920

educational work, because the Germans had closed his school. One day, some Germans came at dawn to throw him out of his apartment. They were very brutal, not even letting him pack the items he had readied just in case. He had barely enough time to pour some sugar into a bag before being forced to leave his apartment with just one suitcase. Unfortunately, the suitcase he took with him contained only shirt collars; the shirts themselves had been left behind in another suitcase! He wanted to go back, but the Germans wouldn't let him. Rafał left his home carrying one suitcase and wearing his fur coat, which served him well during the dramatic winters that were to follow.

Despite everything, Rafał was lucky that the Germans "only" uprooted him. Count Kwilecki, who had been Rafał's deputy in 1939, was shot to death in Grodziec. Because of his occupation as a teacher, belonging to the intelligentsia, his rank of officer, and his participation in the September Campaign, Rafał should have faced the same fate as Count Kwilecki. So, his removal was a satisfactory way out.

There were many Germans living among the Poles in Greater Poland and some of them took revenge against the Poles following the entrance of the Wehrmacht by informing on them to the occupation authorities. Herman, a German teacher at Rafał's school, personally took part in the expulsion of his former principal.

The Germans banished him in the winter of 1940 and, like thousands of other Poles from Wielkopolska, he ended up in the Generalgouvernement. At first, he arrived in Łąkta Górna, south of Bochnia. Later, he moved to Koszyce on the Vistula, where he worked as a teacher in a trade school. It was then that he reached Jędrzejów, taught in the agricultural school in nearby Skroniów, and took up residence with us.

I wasn't very happy that, of all the rooms in our house, my grandparents assigned him my room. I suggested to my grandparents that the new tenant take up residence in the storeroom, which was no longer in use, but Rafał refused. I was very upset that someone new—and a stranger to boot—should occupy my beloved room. I told Grandmother that I couldn't even look at this gentleman.

My cousin Regina and her children helped me empty the room of my belongings. We used the opportunity to wreak havoc on the room and knocked some holes into the walls. I was supposed to move into some tiny room and was very indignant. "He is such a nice man and you are just a troublemaker," Grandmother yelled at me. In any event, Rafał Kałowski started living in my grandparents' house, in my room, in the spring of 1941.

On one occasion I suffered from a terrible toothache and Rafał told my grandmother that he had an effective remedy, some kind of potion, that he could give me. I, however, replied that I didn't want his help and would take nothing from him. Rafał Kałowski was very kind to me, whereas my behavior was the opposite.

When Grandmother baked a cake before *Shabbat*, she would take some to Rafał, while saying to me, "There is a war going on, he has been expelled and lives here all by himself, he also needs help." Grandmother liked Rafał a lot, as did Grandfather. Rafał would often sit with Grandfather and they would become immersed in long conversations. They shared many interests and liked to discuss army issues, the course of the war, and politics.

I kept on being unkind to him and did everything I could to annoy him. He, on the other hand, always behaved like a gentleman towards me, greeting me politely and trying to talk to me. My grandparents knew that, despite my sulking, Rafał was very fond of me and was always kind.

On another occasion, Rafał stood at the entrance to my grandparents' house while I hovered nearby. He addressed me, saying that he fancied one of the local girls. "Take a guess," he said. "Which one would that be?"

"Perhaps Hela?" I asked, thinking of a very good-looking Polish girl who had been expelled from the Poznań region.

"No, no," he replied.

"Then, perhaps Julia?" I replied, thinking of a girl who lived in the neighborhood.

"No," he replied, "not her."

"Do I know her?" I asked.

"Oh, Miss Rózia knows her very well," he said. He didn't tell me who the girl was. He just looked at me and smiled.

A little alley led to my grandparents' house with two lawns on either side of the path—both had dark violet Turkish lilacs as well as some other flowers; the lilac branches partially covered my window. I loved these plants, but when they bloomed, usually passersby would pick some. A beautiful walnut tree also grew under my window, which had been planted by Heniek years before. Once, when I was in the garden, Rafał came in from the alley and said to me, "I would jump into a fire for you, Miss Rózia."

"Well, you can jump, but without me," I retorted.

One day, I was standing with some girlfriends, including Tola Grzywnowicz and Kazia Plucianka, when we saw Rafał on his way back home, swinging his briefcase. He was obviously pleased to see me. "Oh, it's wonderful that I have met Miss Rózia. We can go home together," he said. But I was quite brazen, turned my back on him, and started walking in the opposite direction. All the girls witnessed this affront. Even though I was also on my way home, for some reason I didn't want to go with him. Rafał, who was an ambitious young man, was rightly offended by my behavior. He was clearly upset, but continued on his way without saying a word. From then on, whenever he saw me, he didn't bow to me and left the room whenever I entered. When he saw me coming his way, he would cross over to the other side of the street. Grandmother was quick to notice this change in his behavior and asked me, "What have you done, you urchin?"

"I don't care about him," I replied with bravado. Grandmother kept asking me what I had done, clearly annoyed.

Rafał Kałowski with pupils, c. 1932

To somehow make ends meet, Rafał engaged in a little black market trading. He had some contacts in Kraków, where he traveled now and then. On one occasion he brought back a pair of women's shoes, which Grandmother wanted to buy from him, "Who do you want to buy them for?" he asked.

"For Rózia," Grandmother replied.

"In that case," he said, "I won't sell. She is too much of a lady." And he didn't sell them. This thing that I had done in the presence of my girlfriends must have humiliated him to the core.

At that time, Rafał Kałowski was about 50 years old. He was a grown man, whereas I was just a snotty-nosed kid who had caused him unpleasantness in front of others. He certainly must have felt offended when a spring chicken like me rejected him in such a manner. It was like a rebuke to his behavior towards me, which had always been very gentlemanly.

At that time I was still very immature; when my other girlfriends began looking at and chasing boys, I felt no desire to do the same. This was how my grandparents brought me up. I was tight with my girlfriends, but avoided boys. However, this, of course, did not explain my behavior toward Rafał.

THE GHETTO

In the spring of 1940, the Germans established a closed ghetto within an area of several streets in Jędrzejów, which they isolated from the rest of town. There were constant arrests, especially among the local intelligentsia. It was slightly calmer on the outskirts of town where my grandparents lived, but in town life grew more and more difficult and dangerous.

The Germans behaved like lords of the manor, who could do anything with impunity, and grew more and more brutal and beastly. One of them, by the name of Kap, was particularly savage. Whenever he went out, everyone knew that someone would be his victim. In the morning he would kill some Jew or beggar on the street, and only then would he go back to his place and start his breakfast. He was a total sadist.

Finally, the partisans decided to put an end to it. Late in the summer of 1941 they kidnapped Kap and another Nazi, led them out of town, and killed them both. In reprisal, the Germans arrested ten members of the intelligentsia and shot them to death. Innocent people paid with their lives for Kap's death.

Usually this was the way those things happened: In reprisal for some partisan operation, the Germans would arrest some people and shoot them to death. The best outcome was when the occupiers did not find the body of the person liquidated by the underground, in which case the reprisals were less bloody.

The Germans concentrated the Jews from the town and the environs, including the Jews from Sędziszów, in the Jędrzejów ghetto. In May 1942, right after Passover, we were also expelled to the ghetto. We had to leave the house with nothing except some clothes and a few other essential items. The entire operation was very quick. The Germans came with an order to move us into the ghetto right away. I was at Tola's house at the time. My brother Israel came running to fetch me, saying that the Germans had come and we had to leave the house right away. Shocked and overcome by fear, I quickly returned to my grandparents' house. My father was sitting dispirited in the kitchen, as if he knew where all this was headed. He saw me and started telling me which people he had left some things with for safekeeping. Subconsciously I knew why he was telling me this, but I didn't want to and couldn't accept this. "I don't want to survive either," I sobbed.

The evacuation took place in the evening. The Germans surrounded the house, shouting orders about what to bring with us. They let us pile our things onto a cart hitched to a horse. Not much could be placed on the cart, only the most necessary items. Everything else was left behind—livestock, furniture, agricultural equipment, tools, cooking utensils, and such like. We were then escorted to the ghetto. Our neighbors, the Taboreks, a Polish family with ten or even twelve children, came out of their house and watched the events. I had gone to school with one daughter, Jula, and her brother Antoś. All of them were shocked by our drama. Genia, another daughter, already married, who lived in Warsaw but had returned home with her husband for the duration of the war, started crying.

A neighbor named Gorczak arrived with the Germans. Gorczak had come to Jędrzejów from Poznań, together with some other refugees. It turned out, however, that he was a *Volksdeutsche* (ethnic German) and an informer and everyone thought him a villain. As we were being evacuated, he came up to Genia and, striking her with his hunting crop, he shouted, "What are you crying for?!! For the Jews?!! You pity them?!!"

In the meantime, the Germans kept urging us on, shouting all the time. It was then that Grandmother decided that she should perhaps try to hide somewhere with me. It was an impulsive decision, because no one could even imagine such a possibility. The Germans didn't notice our escape and kept goading on the remaining residents of our house.

It was a miserable sight—the shouts of the Nazis, the silence and sorrow of the adults, the crying of the children, the sympathy of the neighbors. Aunt Leszczyńska told me later that my grandfather had come out of his house wearing a black festive coat, holding a cane, and walking calmly and majestically. He stopped in front of the house, bowed his head, and kissed the ground. He knew he was leaving that place forever.

While the Germans were driving everyone forward to the ghetto, Grandmother and I remained hidden. We snuck away in the darkness, so that no one would notice, in the direction of a Polish family we knew well because they often came to our store. The woman also helped Grandmother take care of the vegetable garden and Grandmother often helped them because they were poor. It was after dusk when we sneaked into a small room attached to their house and spent the night there without telling the owners.

When Grandmother recovered somewhat from the emotions generated by our escape, she started talking to herself and lamenting, "What have I done? We must stay together and go together. Grandfather and I have been living together for so many years."

We sat in this tiny room nestled against each other. She cried and lamented and we talked all night long. She kept repeating, "Perhaps you'll survive." At that time, she didn't know what was going to happen. No one knew then what fate awaited the Jews. But she had a suspicion. "Perhaps Mrs. Leszczyńska would be able to help you. Perhaps Kałowski will take care of you, but I would prefer Mrs. Leszczyńska," she kept on saying with quiet hope. We stayed in the room all night, freezing cold and not sleeping. Our escape was impulsive, sudden and unplanned. It made no sense and Grandmother decided that we would return to the ghetto early in the morning, to stay together with the family.

In the morning we were completely exhausted, so Grandmother knocked on a Polish woman's door and asked her to give us something to drink. Needless to say, the woman started complaining, saying that she was afraid, she had a family, and so on. She didn't give us even a glass of water. For years, whenever she had come to the store, Grandmother used to put all kinds of groceries into her basket, knowing that the woman was very poor. In any event, we turned around without saying a word. And then this woman started running after us, calling to us to leave her the fur coat. I got terribly upset and shouted, "It's better for us to burn it! And you won't get it! You think that if we are going to our deaths, you want us to leave something to you?"

I turned to Grandmother, saying, "Don't give anything to this woman, she's not worth it."

It was just as well we had not asked this woman's permission to spend another night in her shack, because she wouldn't have let us stay and things could have been worse. We walked to the ghetto terribly tired after a sleepless night and humiliated by our meeting and conversation with this woman who Grandmother had hoped would help us, and who hadn't even given us a glass of water.

We settled into the ghetto, living in a completely new situation. The ghetto area was bounded by several streets, such as Łysakowska and Pińczowska. The ghetto was not closed, but guards were posted on the outskirts. All of us went to live at the house of Grandfather's sister, Hendla Fajgenblat. She had a large house, but many people had already settled there and the place got terribly crowded. Father and his family settled somewhere else. After all, Hendla was not a relative of his and also there was not enough space for him and his family.

The Fajgenblats had a bakery and they were still baking bread at the beginning of the war. However, by the time the ghetto was established, the bakery had already been idle for a while. After moving to the ghetto, everything that had existed before ended—study groups, girlfriends, and the protected remains of normal life. Only the ghetto existed and life in it was getting more and more difficult, with an atmosphere of mounting hopelessness and fear.

We celebrated the Sabbath, keeping the hope of survival alive. A Judenrat was set up to administer Jewish affairs. Germans recruited men for various work tasks. Jews were shot to death under any pretext. There was nothing left in the ghetto and life there became impossible. We lived on food purchased outside the ghetto, or on items that someone brought from town, while risking his life. Tola and Rafał Kałowski often brought us food, which was kept in a safe place.

September 1942 was beautiful weather—sunny and balmy but the warm summer was coming to an end. We celebrated the Jewish New Year, *Rosh Hashanah,* with some kind of hope against the brutal reality. We went together to the prayer house on Pińczowska Street, within the ghetto. Everybody prayed fervently for survival. One could hear weeping and heartrending Psalms. However, shortly after *Yom Kippur*, which that year fell on September 20, disaster struck—the Germans liquidated the ghetto. Two, perhaps three days before the liquidation, the Germans arrived from Kielce demanding ransoms and taking bribes. People gave the remains of their property—carpets, gold, and other valuable items—in the hope that perhaps this tribute would postpone the liquidation.

Two days prior to the liquidation, my younger brother, Alter Hil, went outside to get something to eat. He brought back some potatoes and other food. Two days later it was my turn to go on a food expedition. Rafał Kałowski came to us and said he would be waiting for me at the ghetto border.

The Germans let Rafał continue living in our house, but, as was their habit, they also sought a Polish family to settle in the abandoned house, too. Who volunteered? No decent person, for sure. We trusted the Krzysztofiks and thought that perhaps they would take up residence in our house, which would then remain in good hands. But they refused, because their conscience wouldn't let them take possession of our property after our resettlement in the ghetto. Many others also refused, even though their own houses were much smaller. Decent and noble people did not want to get rich on our misery and tragedy.

But there were also others. One person who came to our house was Wawrzyniec Wesołowski, who was known as Wawrzek. He had a brother, no better than he was. Wesołowski was not a native of Jędrzejów. He was a mean person, also toward the Poles, and people hid from him out of fear of being denounced to the Germans. At the first opportunity, he seized the chance to take possession of our house and the family of his niece or nephew settled there. Wesołowski had a house of his own, as well as two cows, other livestock, a thresher, and other farming equipment. He wasn't poor, but nevertheless, he took over our house and removed everything that still remained—livestock, farming machinery, furniture, and cooking utensils. Witnesses told us of his shameless looting.

The night Rafał was due to come near the ghetto I was also supposed to pick up some food from our acquaintances who lived outside of town. But one of the adults stopped me and told me to go the following night. The next day Tola came to us and said that she had been told by members of the underground that the Germans intended to liquidate the ghetto. Everyone laughed at her and not believing her asked, "What are you talking about? The Germans were here several days ago to pick up their ransoms, which we gave them. Now the depopulation of the ghetto is postponed and we have several months of peace. The Germans told us themselves." No one believed her. Tola had come to warn us of the possible liquidation of the ghetto and to look for Heniek because he planned to escape the moment "resettlement" was imminent. But she didn't find him, because he had already snuck out of town.

It was well known, because it had happened several times before, that if one of us didn't show up for an agreed meeting, then Rafał would wait in the same place the next evening. When darkness fell, I put on a thin coat and left the ghetto to meet him. I had barely stepped outside when someone said, "Perhaps you should go tomorrow."

I replied, "But he waited last night and he will be waiting again today. I must go." I had decided and said goodnight to the neighbor.

I left the ghetto at about 8 p.m. Leaving the ghetto in the evening or at night usually involved sleeping over at someone's place. First, I went to the

Krzysztofiks, who usually had some food prepared. They told me that a rumor was making the rounds in town about the imminent liquidation of the ghetto. "What are you talking about?" I asked. "Nothing is going on, the ghetto is peaceful."

From the Krzysztofik's I went to the Leszczyński's where I stayed the night, because it was too late to go anywhere else. In the morning I went to our house to meet Rafał, who had already prepared food for us. I didn't see Rafał in his room, the same room I used to live in, because he had gone to the school in Skroniów where he taught. I decided to wait for him.

Suddenly, Mrs. Leszczyńska came running in. Choking back tears she said quickly, "For heaven's sake, Rózia, don't go anywhere, the ghetto is being liquidated!" It is difficult to find the appropriate words, but I was stunned. I sat by the window and in front of me I looked at Heniek's walnut tree, the lilac bushes, and flowers, and I was simply petrified. Everything was spinning. This was the end. It was expected, but still it was sudden. After a while, I broke down and started wailing, "I want to go. I want to go to them!"

This was my first, quite natural impulse—to be with one's own, together, even in death. Mrs. Leszczyńska hugged me, covered me with a shawl, and took me to her place. I left our house—now it would never be ours. She led me along the garden path and left me among the raspberry bushes, because she didn't want to tell her family and the domestics about my presence. She said, "Sit down here, wait, perhaps we'll learn something. Where would you go, my child? Where? I don't know. Over there everyone is being hustled to the train."

Rafał also learned quickly about the liquidation of the ghetto. One of Tola's brothers rode to get him from school. He returned home right away. He missed me and contacted Tola and Mrs. Leszczyńska, who told him about my whereabouts. They quickly gathered some food and homemade wine and Tola and her brothers rode their bicycles to the train station in the hope of giving the provisions to my family. But all they managed to do was bring news about the operation of liquidating the ghetto.

The Germans had surrounded the ghetto before dawn and immediately started chasing people out of their homes to the market square, which adjoined Łysakowska Street all the way down to the ghetto border. The Jews stood packed next to each other on the square. My older brother, Israel, scared out of his wits, pressed himself against Grandmother, and my younger brother, Alter, held her hand. A German walked up to her and struck her. A moment before, Grandmother had given Heniek her ring and gestured to him that he should edge toward a group of men who had labor certificates. Heniek stayed with his parents until the end and witnessed their last moments, including the humiliation of his mother by the Germans. The cattle cars were already in place and the Nazis brutally chased everyone inside. I listened to all this and wept, "I have nothing to live for anymore! I have lost everyone!" I lamented.

Mrs. Leszczyńska tried to console me, "There is nothing you can do now. Perhaps someone survived."

When everything was over, after the Nazis liquidated the Jędrzejów ghetto at dawn, after everyone was deported to a concentration camp, all my loved ones were gone—my father, brothers, grandparents, relatives, and acquaintances. All the while, I had been hiding at the Leszczyński's. I was in a state of complete shock, numb, petrified. Everything around me seemed as normal, just like before, but for me nothing had the old light, the same gleam, colors or smells.

I looked at my grandparents' house. What was I thinking? I believed, because I was taught to believe, that there is a God, that miracles do happen, but I simply couldn't comprehend anything. The thought that returned obsessively and kept going round in my head was that they couldn't have killed them all, that they were somewhere, they were alive some place, they would return. I simply couldn't accept that this had come to pass.

Why did I have to hide today, to be afraid? I looked through the window and wondered what was going on. It was the same world around me, the same people, but was I the same person? Once, just several days ago, even yesterday, I could still walk around, and now I had to be in hiding. Why? How could they? What for? It was impossible. I prayed within myself. I believed, or perhaps deluded myself, that what had happened would surely be reversed.

In the afternoon, I learned that Heniek had survived and remained in the ghetto. Immediately after the liquidation of the ghetto, the Germans had established the so-called "small ghetto" where nearly 100 people were held, including some Jews who worked on the railroad and had special papers. When the Jews were lined up at the fairground, one of the cousins slipped Heniek a work certificate for work on the railroad. Heniek showed it to the Germans, who told him to cross over to the group that was supposed to stay behind. In addition to the workers on the railroad, members of the so-called Jewish police were also allowed to stay. The news about Heniek's survival helped me to hold out during the first hours of the tragedy. Only two of us remained.

All the Jews from the Jędrzejów ghetto were transported by the Nazis straight to Treblinka. Someone managed to escape and return to Jędrzejów and later told the whole story of how and when the Jędrzejów Jews were exterminated in Treblinka. My entire family, all my loved ones, perished.

Heniek (Henry) Landschaft, 1945

CHAPTER 3

ON THE RUN

LEARNING TO HIDE

I started to hide, or rather, to be hidden, and a new chapter in my life began. I spent the first day on the Leszczyński's estate, although my presence was kept secret from the family and servants. I couldn't spend the night there, so it was decided that in the evening I would move to Tola's house. When darkness fell, Aunt Leszczyńska went with me to Rafał's room at my grandparents' house; I was supposed to wait for him there so he could escort me to Tola's. As I waited I felt crushed by what had happened, by the tragedy of my loved ones and my friends. My world had shattered into a million particles of ash.

Finally, Rafał came and began a serious conversation with me about my future. He confirmed his willingness to take care of me in order to save and protect me. He reminded me that he had made this promise to my grandparents and my father, and stressed that he wished to keep his word and do everything possible to save me. I replied, "I have survived and now I am all by myself, but Heniek, my uncle, my only and closest relative, is also alive. I ask you to take care of him as you are taking care of me, to save both of us. Otherwise, I don't see any point to go on living."

Rafał responded, "Yes, he is as precious to me as you are."

I accepted his proposal, trusting him to do everything possible to save Heniek and me. Under the cover of darkness, he escorted me to Tola's house and left me there for the night.

A rumor started going round Jędrzejów that I had survived. It was possible that someone had seen me sneak through the town the previous night and started the rumor that I had not returned to the ghetto once the liquidation had started.

The rumor also reached the ears of Wawrzek Wesołowski, the man who had "taken over" and looted my grandparents' house. He came there once again and made a thorough search of the entire house, as well as the farmyard, attics, and alcoves and looked everywhere for me, or at least for traces of my presence. He didn't want any witness to, or accuser of, his greed and vileness. People who saw his shameful search told me about it. They also warned me about him. But I wasn't planning to return to our house and meanwhile remained in hiding at Tola's.

A man named Miarecki had served as the Blue Police commandant before the war. He was known for his fondness for bribes. Needless to say, he knew me well as during the occupation, but before the establishment of the ghetto, Tola, Adela, and I had played a little prank on Miarecki: There was a flower bed of pansies in front of the police post and one day we picked some of them, made a little wreath, and tied it to Miarecki's bicycle. Giggling, we hid round the corner waiting for his reaction. But in the meantime, a cleaning woman came by, saw what we had done and shouted, "Mr. Commandant, someone cut flowers and tied them to your bicycle!" In all likelihood, Miarecki must have also learned that I had slipped away.

During my first evening at Tola's, when only the two of us were home (her brothers were somewhere else), we started making preparations for the night. Tola asked me, as if she had had a premonition, "In case someone comes looking for you, what will you do, where will you hide?"

"In a closet," I replied.

We went to bed and a few moments later, while we were still awake, we heard someone knocking on the window. I quickly jumped out of bed and hid in a closet. Escaping outside was not an option. It was Miarecki and, brandishing a rifle, he entered the house, saying, "Well, Miss Tola, have I missed someone? I thought I would meet Miss Rózia here."

Tola said, "What are you talking about? All of them were removed from the ghetto. The Germans chased them to the train and she went with them."

"Really?" he replied. "That's a pity. You were always such good friends. That's too bad. She was so young and pretty."

As he talked he paced back and forth in the room, coming closer to the closet. I was inside, among the clothes, crouching to make myself smaller. I was frightened and stressed and I was cold, because all I was wearing was a nightshirt. In the darkness and congestion of the closet, I wanted to put something on. Then a hanger knocked and something fell, making a noise. "Get out, pussycat! It's the cat," Tola said quickly, keeping her wits about her. Then I started coughing; it's always like that—a cough tends to make itself known especially in such situations. "Dear Lord," I said to myself in despair, "this coughing will be the end of me yet. If he hears me and checks the closet, I will jump out quickly and run away. Hopefully, he won't shoot me."

Miarecki came to Tola's house as if convinced that I might be there. He must have known something as he kept looking everywhere, sniffing around, and asking questions about me. He was a bastard, like many Blue Police there, but he wasn't evil. People knew that all he wanted was a bribe. He probably didn't even want to see me, because then he would have to arrest me and hand me over to the Germans. He liked me; he had gone to my grandparents so many times and had always received something from them. He also warned people off, including Tola's brothers.

He didn't move and kept making small talk and asking questions. Now and then he said, "Pity she had to go with all the others." Meanwhile, I pressed my hand against my mouth to prevent myself from coughing. It seemed to me as if I could hold off no longer.

Finally, Miarecki left and I came out of the closet, choking, and trying to catch my breath. I tried to explain to Tola my thoughtlessness, "What could I do? I was shivering with cold. I thought that somehow I could manage to put something on. But I hit the hanger and it fell."

Miarecki refused to give up and kept Tola's house under surveillance. So although I could remain there, I couldn't stay in the apartment and therefore, I hid in a large barn located in the yard. Tola brought me food and drink. Miarecki's visits became more frequent. He saw Rafał riding his bicycle to visit us; he knew him well from when he started living with us.

Tola's house was surrounded by trees and luxuriant lilac bushes. It was there that Miarecki hid, following the entire goings-on in the house and farmyard. He didn't believe Tola and was perhaps waiting for me to come out. Usually, whenever Tola came to me in the barn with food, Miarecki would immediately pop up nearby. Tola would notice him immediately, saying to me, "Miarecki is coming. I am going home. Quick."

Miarecki didn't talk much, but we could see that he sensed what was going on. After a week of observations and sneaking up on Tola, he came to her and said, without beating around the bush, "Miss Tola, I know everything. Rózia is here. She can't stay. May the devil take Kałowski! I am going to give him business."

He knew about my conflict with Rafał and, during his observations, he had seen Rafał coming often to Tola's house and probably figured out why. Miarecki proclaimed, "I never suspected that Rafał was in love with her. I mean, they didn't talk to each other, they were angry with each other." Rafał did not run into Miarecki in the vicinity of Tola's house, although he knew that the policeman sniffed around.

"She can't stay here," Miarecki said time and again. "It's too bad, she's young, but she must go somewhere else." He even asked Tola whether she protected me out of kindness.

"And what do you think?" Tola asked. "Do you remember when I had an appendix operation already during the war in '41, here in the hospital in Jędrzejów? It was Rózia who came to visit me. She would take off her armband and visit me at great personal risk. She brought me food and cookies. And as for her grandmother? She helped me so much after I became an orphan and had the whole house on my shoulders. No Polish woman helped me as much as Grandmother Landschaft. How could I refuse to reciprocate?"

"Well, it's true that you were very tight, you two," Miarecki reflected. "But that won't count for much."

In any event, at that time, he still could have handed me over to the Germans. That he didn't do so was probably on account of Tola and her brothers, who would have been shot for hiding a Jew. Or, he could have taken me to some field somewhere and killed me, and then said he had run into a Jewish girl. But he didn't hand me over. He just warned Tola, saying he knew I was hiding at her place, and told her to make me disappear. Tola must have given him something for this "favor." She didn't have any valuables, so she probably gave him food.

I stayed in Tola's barn for more than a week after the liquidation of the ghetto. We all thought that it would be safer and more peaceful there than at the Leszczyński's. All of Tola's brothers knew I was hiding there. I knew them well from before the war. Both Heniek and I were very close to them. However, the hiding place at Tola's became "hot" faster than we thought.

So I returned to the Leszczyński's as it was the only place where I could still hide. Fortunately, the Germans had not appropriated their estate, as was their wont. Living there were the Leszczyński couple, their three daughters—my girlfriends—and Aunt Miecia's father, old Płatkowski. There were only two servants—a young woman and Władek Felis, who was later let in on the secret of my hiding there. He was very devoted to his employers and they gave him their full trust.

Rafał visited the ghetto and met Heniek, who was in the group of Jews left in place by the Germans. Also in this group was our cousin, Perla (nee Fajgenblat). Her husband was a ghetto policeman and in cases like this the Germans usually let the spouses stay. Later, both of them ended up in a camp in Częstochowa, but only she survived the war.

During Rafał's visits to the ghetto, he and Heniek deliberated on how to save me. Heniek had to rely on Rafał's help as the residents of the small ghetto were more closely watched, even though the ghetto was still not fenced off. The men worked on the railroad, digging ditches and making ramparts.

After the liquidation of the ghetto, the Germans took every valuable item that remained in the Jewish-owned apartments and put up for sale anything that could still be of use. People from town and the surrounding villages attended the sale out of greed. They made purchases, haggled over prices, and the Germans laughed. Aunt Leszczyńska told me that the priest Marchewka reproached the community during his sermons saying, "People, don't go there, don't buy anything, because those things are stained with blood!" But the people couldn't help themselves and continued taking advantage of the opportunity. The Germans mocked them sarcastically, "So you are pushing and shoving to get the Jews' things. Who will take your things after you are gone?"

Residents of the small ghetto felt that the Germans would soon liquidate it too, and it was unclear what they would do with this group that they had left in the ghetto. In fact, two or three months later, the Germans indeed liquidated the small ghetto. Rafał, who maintained constant contact with Heniek, got him out much earlier, thus saving him from German expulsion. He brought him to Tola's place.

Rafał and Aunt Miecia were aware of the fact that a new place had to be found for me, outside Jędrzejów, because everyone in Jędrzejów knew me and my situation was becoming more and more dangerous. Furthermore, rumors were still making the rounds about my having survived the destruction of the ghetto and staying in town. Rafał kept looking for a suitable and safe hideout and Aryan papers were prepared for me.

IN CHLEWICE—AT THE GRZEGOREK'S AND KITA'S

The village of Chlewice was situated about 23 kilometers from Jędrzejów, on the road to Częstochowa. Rafał knew a family by the name of Grzegorek who had settled in Chlewice, having been uprooted by the Germans from their home in the Poznań region. He went to see them, told them about my situation without hiding the fact that I was Jewish, and proposed that I live at their place for a while. The Grzegoreks agreed.

The Grzegorek family had three children: Heniek, who was younger than me; Jurek, who was the youngest of the three; and a daughter, Halina, who was my age. After arriving in Chlewice they had settled in a house that was previously owned by Jews. They knew Rafał from before the war, because they had lived in Grodziec, where Rafał worked as the school principal. A man named Przeździeń, who had been uprooted from Kalisz, also lived with them. Przeździeń liked to drink.

In order to prepare for my departure, I had to change my appearance somewhat. I had long, beautiful braids, which were dark, but not black. It was decided that they should be trimmed and made lighter using hydrogen peroxide, which would make me look more Aryan. Rafał secured a church certificate for me and a forged baptism certificate was in the works. I was to become a Polish girl, resettled from Greater Poland; there were many such people in the area and, therefore, I would not raise suspicion.

Maryla Leszczyńska gave me a small catechism and I quickly learned the prayers, the principles of faith, and the songs. Learning was easy for me and I remembered even long texts without special effort. I knew all the carols, because we used to sing them during the nativity plays at school before the war and also a little at the Leszczyński's, when their daughters and I dressed the Christmas tree.

My braids were cut and my hair got lighter, which turned out to be our biggest mistake. During the war there was no hair dye to be had and the only means for lightening hair was hydrogen peroxide. But this turned hair rust-red, whereas we had wanted to make it blond, which was illogical anyway since I had dark eyes. Ultimately, we managed to lighten my hair a little and Aunt Leszczyńska gave me an extra bottle of hydrogen peroxide, advising me to put it on my hair at night and in the morning my hair would look all right.

I was ready to move out. I put on the thin coat that I had worn when I left the ghetto. Tola gave me a green hat with a black ribbon to protect me from being recognized, and Aunt Miecia gave me a nightshirt and blouses that belonged to her daughters. In the afternoon, Maryla escorted me from the Leszczyński's to the road. I wore a black crepe armband on my sleeve because in Chlewice I was supposed to say that I was grieving for my brother who had died recently. Rafał waited for me by the road to give me a ride on his bicycle to Chlewice.

We arrived after a long journey of 25 kilometers and reached the Grzegorek's in the evening. Rafał introduced me to them and left immediately. I remained alone. Before going to bed, I put hydrogen peroxide once again on my hair, in accordance with Aunt Leszczyńska's instructions. Halinka Grzegorek, whom I had just met, helped me with the task. I woke up in the morning, looked in the mirror, and was rooted to the spot with fright. My hair had turned rusty-red and I looked like a crimson chicken! I felt so helpless I wept. If I had stopped after the first time, it would have looked tolerable, but now it was a disaster and I was heartbroken. This wretched hair also made a terrible impression on the Grzegorek family.

All these new events, tragic and dramatic, took place in September and October—moving from house to house, from the Leszczyński's to Tola's, and back again, the decision to leave Jędrzejów, making the preparations for moving, and Rafał's efforts to secure Aryan papers; the hiding, fear, and anxiety, along with Miarecki's forays; and the loneliness, hopelessness, risk-taking, and relying only on the help of others. I had to overcome and deal with all these experiences, while all the time having the shadow of the tragedy of my loved ones, the deaths of the people closest to me, hanging over me.

All I had with me was the forged baptism certificate issued in the name of Mieczysława Borowska, who allegedly had been born somewhere in Greater Poland and was deported to the Generalgouvernment. As Rafał had been unable to arrange a forged *kenkarte* (identification card) for me, I submitted my certificate and fingerprints to the village council office. The procedure of issuing a *kenkarte* was very long, taking two or even three months, and I had to get hold of a resident's permit for Chlewice. A young clerk helped me solve these problems.

I spent only a few days with the Grzegorek family. My situation quickly became very difficult as it turned out that Mr. Grzegorek was a coward. The Germans arrived in Chlewice and began a roundup, abducting young men and women for forced labor. The village residents were afraid, as was Grzegorek. I had a cold at that time, probably after the night journey by bicycle from Jędrzejów to Chlewice, and was in bed when I heard Grzegorek enter the house and say to his wife, "Little Mama, listen, perhaps we should take her somewhere." He never addressed her by her name, only "Mama" or "Little Mama." Frightened, I listened to the conversation, wondering how it would end.

I got up and was informed that I had to leave and would be taken to a man named Kita. Escorted by Grzegorek and Przeździeń, I covered my head with a shawl to hide my red hair and look more adult. Darkness had already fallen and Grzegorek, who was frightened out of his wits, wanted to leave me on the outskirts of the village, so that I would go by myself to this Kita person, whom I didn't know of course. But Przeździeń intervened saying, "Mr. Grzegorek, we can't do this. If she goes there by herself, they won't take her in! Kałowski left her with us. We can't just abandon her!" But Grzegorek wasn't convinced. His fear was stronger than he was and he went back home, leaving me with Przeździeń. He knocked on the door of Kita's cottage and called, "Mr. Kita, Mr. Kita, this is Przeździeń, open up!"

Nothing happened for a long while. Night had already fallen and all the lights inside the cottage were out. Maybe they were asleep. Finally, Kita opened the door, looked around, and saw Przeździeń, whom he knew. He asked, "What's going on? We locked the door because all kinds of things are happening. You never know who'll knock on your door. Come on in." Well, this was an unexpected welcome. Had I gone to Kita by myself he might have refused me entry, chased me away, or perhaps even informed the authorities that a strange girl, Jewish of course, was somewhere in the area. But he opened the door for Przeździeń because he knew him.

Przeździeń introduced me to them, saying, "This is my niece from Kalisz who arrived here earlier today. Now there is a roundup going on and young people are being taken away to Germany. All I need is for her to be rounded up too. Why don't you shelter her for a few days? Let her stay for a few days. She can help around the house."

"OK, she can stay," said both Kita and his wife.

We entered the main room and Przeździeń introduced me to them. They made a bed for me on the floor. Exhausted by all this tension I slept like a log. Przeździeń went back home and the next day he cycled to Rafał to tell him about the new developments and lay out my situation.

The Kitas lived some distance from the village with only a few small farmyards set off from each other. There was only one room in their cottage and everyone slept and ate there, including Kita's old father. The cabin, the barn, and the yard were very run down and neglected.

I arrived at their place late in the evening on Saturday. The next day Mrs. Kita made chicken soup. When you make chicken soup, the scum, which always rises to the surface is collected and thrown away. At least this is what Grandmother always did. But the Kita woman gathered this scum and added it to our soup. I saw this and felt nauseous. I was hungry, but told myself that I wouldn't eat it.

I sat for a while in the kitchen to warm myself. It was cold in the room, but only my head was covered in order to hide my face and my wretched red hair. Kita's wife noticed this and said, "You are so young! You must have been born during a harsh winter if you are so cold." I nodded in assent. Slowly, step by step, I began playing a game at not being myself in order to save myself. These were the first days full of new experiences and I had no idea where they would lead me.

Unfortunately, it turned out that Kita knew my "hometown" of Kalisz a little because he had once served in the army there. He started telling me about the town that I had never visited and asking me how things were there now. I gave noncommittal replies and somehow I emerged from this incident unscathed. Old Kita was a folk poet and kept on showering us with rhymes such as, "Warsaw and Kraków are the Poles' capitals / Kielce and Jędrzejów are the thieves' capitals."

Beyond the Kita family's potato field stretched their neighbor's farm. They told me that rich peasants lived there and they had a young son. Kita walked up to me and said, "This young neighbor says that a pretty girl is staying with us. 'Perhaps,' he said, 'I could be introduced to her and marry her.' He is rich, why don't you marry him?"

"I can't," I replied. "I left my fiancé in Kalisz."

Rafał arrived the next day, after Przeździeń notified him about the developments and together with the Grzegorek family they started looking for a suitable place for me to stay. After two nights at Kita's place, Rafał and Przeździeń came to pick me up. Old Kita was very curious about everything and started asking Rafał about me—where I was from, when I was born, and so on. He expressed his astonishment that I was so young and already had a fiancé in Kalisz.

AT BEDNARSKA'S

On the outskirts of the village stood the cabin of the widow Bednarska, who lived there with her two children and her mother. Rafał and the Grzegorek woman decided to approach her. Rafał described the situation to Bednarska and, referring to me as his niece, asked her whether I could live at her place. He said he would pay for rent and food and would come to visit from time to time to make sure everything was all right. And so I began living at Bednarska's in late October. I remember All Saints' Day was on November 1 that year and I went with her to the cemetery to visit the grave of her little son. To Bednarska I was Miss Dzidka. I used this name all the time, in every situation, and in the course of my new and incessant changes in lodgings. When asked about my name I would reply that my true name was Mieczysława, but I had been nicknamed Dzidka since early childhood. This permanent, everyday name also gave me protection, because it helped me not to get confused in front of strangers, since my official papers changed many times. Even today some people still address me as Dzidka.

True to his word Rafał came to visit me once a week and paid Bednarska for my upkeep. Her cabin was located close to a forest, on a side road, some distance away from the main thoroughfare that passed through the village.

Both Bednarska and her daughter tilled the field that stretched beyond the cabin.

It was peaceful at Bednarska's even though they were poverty-stricken. Usually, we had very little to eat; there was no bread, now and then there were pancakes baked on a hot plate, but mostly we lived on potatoes and a thin soup. Bednarska's two children were Danusia, a girl of about 10 or 11, and Januszek, a son of about five. Her husband had apparently perished in Auschwitz, or at least this was the news she had received about him.

I took care of the children a bit and helped with the cleaning and cooking. When Rafał came to visit I noticed that Bednarska flirted with him a little. Rafał also noticed. She was still young and pretty and Rafał was handsome and good-looking. However, I knew that Bednarska noticed that Rafał preferred to look at me, because once she said to the Grzegorek couple, "Kałowski looks at Miss Dzidka as if she were a painting."

Bednarska's mother would make anti-Jewish statements now and then. Once we were talking about Jews and her mother summed up the conversation by saying, "They did well by those lice that they eradicated them." In moments such as these I had to remain sanguine and couldn't let anything show. On the contrary, I had to take part in the conversation in order not to expose myself. When jokes were being told, including anti-Jewish ones, I had to take part in the fun.

A partisan by the name of Stanisław Limanowski visited Bednarska's cabin now and then. He was 26 or 27 and very tall and handsome. Limanowski was supposed to be engaged to Bednarska's younger sister, who lived someplace else.

Bednarska had just one room with a clay ceiling. Her old mother slept in one bed with Januszek, Bednarska slept with her daughter in a second bed, and I had a bed of my own. The beds were lined up against the walls of the cabin. In one corner stood a closet, which was always set off a little from the wall. Limanowski slept in the attic and whenever someone came to visit, he hid behind the closet.

The first time Limanowski came after my arrival, I was already in bed. Bednarska opened the door and when he came inside he turned on his flashlight and surveyed the room. He noticed me and asked, "Hela, who do you have here? Perhaps you are hiding some Jews?"

"No," she replied. "This is Dzidka from the Poznań region."

In the morning, on seeing me and my wretched dyed hair he said, "I know that Miss Dzidka is in hiding. Next time I come I will bring Miss Dzidka some oak leaves from the forest. When the hair is washed with them it will change its color. I also did this," he added. He didn't say anything else, but could he have guessed something? He spent that day with us and told us about himself—he was with partisans in the woods and the Germans were already looking for him. When I made the beds in the morning I noticed a revolver, which he had left under his pillow.

In the afternoon I went to the Grzegoreks and told them that a partisan was frequenting Bednarska's cabin and that I had also seen his gun. I wanted them and Rafał to know about it because Limanowski's visits to Bednarska increased the risk involved in my staying there.

I don't know whether he suspected that I was Jewish. Perhaps he guessed something. It wasn't likely that I was hiding for any other reason, such as political. But he stressed that he was also hiding and that in this regard our situation was similar.

A week later Limanowski came again, this time in the morning and he spent the whole day with us. He said goodbye in the evening, saying he was going back to the forest for the night, but it didn't turn out like that.

Meanwhile, Rafał smuggled Heniek out of the ghetto because of persistent rumors that the Germans intended to liquidate the small ghetto, though it wasn't clear what they would do with the remaining Jews. In fact, in February 1943 the Germans indeed liquidated the ghetto and transferred its "residents" to the ammunition factory in Skarżysko and to a camp in Częstochowa.

Rafał was looking for a safe hideout for Heniek, beyond Jędrzejów, because Tola's house was partially "hot" after my stay there, and besides, everyone in Jędrzejów knew him. Because of the dangers to Tola and her brothers, there was no way he could stay there for much longer. Rafał talked to the Grzegoreks about Heniek living with them under the guise of a distant relative from Wielkopolska.

It was late October, cold and muddy. At first, Rafał intended to bring me to Tola to see Heniek, but finally he decided that we should go first to the Leszczyński's. He was already very tired and the Leszczyński estate was closer, and also it seemed safer.

Aunt Miecia was glad to see me and I stayed there for the night. Mr. Leszczyński knew that I had arrived unexpectedly that evening, escorted by Rafał, to spend the night. He took fright, and kept asking his wife, "When will she leave? When will she leave? When?" In contrast to his wife he was very fearful and didn't get involved in her undertakings. He was much older than her, about 60 at the time, whereas she was 35. Mieczysława married when she was barely 18, immediately upon graduation from high school. Leszczyński was a rich landowner and owned a large estate, but before long the estate went into decline and the farm fell into more and more debt. They also had another farm of about 68 hectares.

At dawn I returned to Grandfather's house and waited there for Rafał, who was to escort me to Tola's house. With great emotion and pain I remembered the life in this house where I had never felt lonely but loved, and where the drama of our family began. The family of Wesołowski's brother lived in another part of the house, at the other end of the hallway.

I spent the day in Rafał's room in a prepared hideout behind the cupboard, which could be entered by removing a wooden plank. Rafał came in the afternoon and said, "You know what happened? Today Leszczyński had a heart attack, fell on the ground in the garden, and died on the spot." Towards evening he took me to Tola's house where I spent the night and Rafał returned to his place.

Shortly afterwards, Tola's house became too dangerous for Heniek to stay there. Rafał secured a forged baptism certificate for him and pleaded with the Grzegoreks to take him in. Apart from that unfortunate incident when Grzegorek Senior panicked and sent me to the Kita family, relations with them were very good. They, too, knew who Heniek truly was and that we were relatives. Heniek began sharing my fate of life in hiding, in constant flight, and in fear of his life.

Heniek arrived in Chlewice as Mr. Stanisław Łobodarski. He took up residence in the Grzegorek's house and immediately submitted his documents to the village administration office in order to gain a resident's permit and *kenkarte*. Officially, we didn't know each other and knew nothing about each other. When I happened to be at the Grzegorek's house, we were very aloof toward each other, like strangers. It helped that we didn't resemble each other physically—I had more Semitic features with dark hair and eyes, nose shape, and face, whereas Heniek, although dark, did not look Jewish.

Sometimes, the Grzegorek woman would make plans. "When the war is over we will marry all of you. You, Henio," she said about her son, "will get together with Dzidka, and Stasiek with our Halinka. That's what we'll do, after we are finished with hiding them."

One evening, after the partisan Limanowski had spent the whole day with us at Bednarska's house, I had a sense of foreboding, which I don't understand even today, and I asked little Danusia to sleep next to me that night. I don't know what came over me, because I always slept alone, whereas the children slept with their mother and grandmother. Danusia slept in my bed with me on the wall side.

That night Germans and Blue Police approached Bednarska's house and began surrounding it. I woke up to the sound of German and Polish being spoken and was petrified, but there was nothing I could do. At that time I didn't have my *kenkarte* yet, or any other document for that matter; I had submitted my certificate to the village administration office immediately after arrival in Chlewice and was awaiting my *kenkarte*.

Germans and Blue Police! I rose from the bed for a moment. The Bednarski women also woke up and the old woman turned to me, trying to cheer me up, "It's nothing, Miss Dzidka." They, too, were scared by this nighttime raid. They didn't know my true identity and guessed that this raid was related to the search for Limanowski.

The bed on which I slept was filled with straw, countryside fashion. I turned toward the wall and pressed myself against it, burying myself in and covering myself with the eiderdown. I didn't want to think or see anything—it was one of those completely terrifying moments in one's life. I heard the Germans and Blue Police enter the house and heard their conversations in German and Polish.

I realized that they were looking for Limanowski. It turned out that he had spent the night in the attic and hadn't gone back to the woods. Someone must have informed on him. When some of the raiders entered the cabin, Limanowski jumped out of the attic, started shooting, and fled to the woods without his shoes. The Germans also started shooting but their fire was ineffective.Then they started asking about Limanowski. One of them sat on the edge of my bed next to Danusia and asked her, "Who was that gentleman? What was he doing in the attic? Whose shoes are those?" By a stroke of luck they had found his shoes in the attic rather than in the main room.

"I don't know, I know nothing," Danusia replied sleepily.

She was resolute and smart. She didn't divulge anything despite the tricky questions. At the same time as asking questions, they searched the house and the main room. They were looking for any traces of Limanowski—personal items, weapons, etc. They talked among themselves about a briefcase and some bandits, by which they meant partisans. They rooted behind the closet, which stood right next to my bed. Someone looked under the bed where I lay, lifted the eiderdown, and felt around with his hands. They searched in every place possible. They didn't try to chase Limanowski as it was futile and besides, they feared the forest at night, so they got busy with the cabin, suspecting they would find something there.

I lay motionless, feeling as if I wanted to be absorbed by the wall. It was dark in the cabin, but they lit a lamp and had flashlights. They kept asking who was there, referring all the time to this "bandit" who had slipped away. It never occurred to them that there was someone else in the cabin besides the Bednarski family. They saw the old woman sleeping in the same bed as her young grandchild, a second bed with the young mother, and a third bed with a ten-year-old girl and someone else, probably her sister. They must have noticed me, but didn't wake me up. I wonder why.

Also, luckily for us, little Januszek slept throughout this operation, and it didn't occur to the policemen to wake him up. It was astonishing that the little boy was not awakened by the noise, the shooting, the yelling or the light in the room. Had Januszek woken up or had they woken him up and started questioning him, as they did Danusia, he would have told them everything, because he was too young to keep his wits about him as his older sister had.

Had they woken me up and started asking me questions, I would have surely been a goner. But I was saved from what seemed like a helpless situation. They took Bednarska to the police station, but later let her go because she managed to talk her way out of the predicament she was in. They didn't find anything during the search to indicate the presence of the partisan. She explained that she didn't know about his coming to her cabin, that he must have climbed to the attic undetected. Somehow she prevailed.

The next morning, I felt as if I had been on another planet, to a different world, my life having started again from the beginning. I was barely conscious after a night filled with fear, emotions, and sleeplessness. The foreboding, which then, unconsciously, had told me to ask Danusia to sleep next to me, and her presence in my bed, probably saved my life. I had a sense of foreboding on many future occasions, and it usually preceded sudden and dramatic situations in which I later found myself.

Danusia told the whole story to Januszek saying, "They asked me who was there. I told them. 'I don't know, I don't know.' He asked, 'Was he your papa or mama's fiancé?' And I kept repeating, 'I don't know, I don't know anything.'"

"I would have said that it was Mr. Stasio," replied Januszek.

Well, we were very, very lucky that he had slept and the policemen hadn't woken him up. He would have "sung" about Limanowski, his mother, and myself.

I went to see the Grzegorek family to give them an account of this nighttime drama, because they were the only ones who were in on my story and situation. Heniek—Mr. Stasio—was there too and also heard my story.

The Grzegorek couple notified Rafał about the incident. He arrived almost immediately and together they decided that my continued stay at Bednarska's involved too many risks. The village residents knew about some girl named Dzidka living at Bednarska's. I moved about the village, and although not too much in order to avoid attention, I simply couldn't spend the whole day locked up in the cabin. However, being in the same village all the time was very risky and imprudent, but then no one had expected this and besides, there were no other possibilities for hiding me.

I had to be constantly prepared for a new life, not knowing that "new" would repeat itself many times, without warning, forcing me to sever all ties. It was now obvious to us that I had to move to another apartment and the Grzegorek woman volunteered to search for a new abode.

The story with my hair was not yet over. Just as he had promised during his first visit to Bednarska's, when he was introduced to me, Limanowski had brought me oak leaves so that I could make a brew and rinse my rusty-red hair with it. I did as I was told, hoping my hair would regain its natural color, but the opposite happened. After rinsing my hair in the oak leaf brew, it came out green! It was a nightmare. It looked comical, but I wanted to cry. I hid my hair under a kerchief and vowed to just let it grow back. I didn't want to experiment anymore. Besides everyone had got used to my whimsical ways.

Officially, I was a resettled person from Wielkopolska. However, now and then, some people either told me directly or repeated to me what they had heard—that this Dzidka girl has hair similar to a Jewish girl who had lived in Chlewice before the war. I would reply that I liked blond hair, that I had wanted to brighten it with hydrogen peroxide, but it hadn't worked.

Several days after the incident at Bednarska's house, a rumor started going around the village, fortunately in my favor, saying, "This Dzidka who was at Bednarska's had some dealings with Limanowski." Because I moved out of Bednarska's house shortly after the raid, people made a connection between the two events. I spent about two months living at Bednarska's, but new developments forced me to move again.

AT PAWLIKOWA'S

The Grzegorek woman quickly found a new place for me, and two days after this memorable night I started living at Pawlikowa's. She was 26 and had a six-year-old daughter, named Marysia. Pawlikowa used to say that she was a widow, but after the war it turned out that her husband had been a Polish soldier who returned to Chlewice after the war. Pawlikowa's father, Czajkowski, lived with her and her daughter. He worked as a carpenter and kept bees. Her two brothers also lived in Chlewice. Leon, the younger one, had a fiancée in the village.

Pawlikowa's house had one room and a kitchen and stood facing the road. I shared a bed with Marysia, Pawlikowa had the second bed to herself, and her father slept in the kitchen.

While at Pawlikowa's I used to clean the entire house, as she preferred to visit other village women to gossip. When someone visited her, the guest would immediately notice that the house was clean and had been spruced up, and would praise my work. I also whitened the living room floor with lime.

Pawlikowa knew how to knit pretty things and taught me how to knit. Leon was involved in illegal livestock butchery, so now and then he would bring his sister and father some scraps of pork. The poverty and hunger that plagued Bednarska's house was not to be found here.

Needless to say, I wasn't used to eating pork. My grandparents' kitchen was kosher, of course, and I simply couldn't get used to this non-kosher meat. My stomach would protest and I would be immediately seized with nausea from the pork fat and cracklings. Also, I couldn't eat potato soup seasoned with fat. However, I couldn't show my revulsion and forced myself to eat at least a little bit. At Pawlikowa's either potato soup or sour soup seasoned with cracklings was served every day. We had meat every now and then, but usually just grease and pork fat.

When I moved into Pawlikowa's house it was the middle of December and Advent season. Pawlikowa started dragging me out of bed in the morning to go to church for early morning Advent mass. She used to yell, "Dzidka, get up for the Advent mass."

"But Mrs. Pawlikowa, I have nothing to put on," I would reply quietly.

It was true. I had neither a winter coat nor thick clothing for the winter. I was going without stockings and it came as no surprise that my feet were frostbitten. Without stockings and wearing only slippers, I would run through the snow. People expressed their astonishment, asking whether I wasn't cold. What could I do?

The church was close by but it was already very cold, especially at dawn, and the church wasn't heated. I tried to talk my way out of attending the service, but Pawlikowa was unyielding, saying, "Get up and come to church." However, on some occasions she would relent and not wake me up.

I was happy with my lodgings because I cleaned the entire house and performed many other household chores, which satisfied Pawlikowa. I also took care of Marysia. I spent quite a lot of time with her and she also got to like me. Pawlikowa liked me, but sometimes she would say, "Our Dzidka is an okay gal. Only she made her hair like some Jewess."

Sometimes something funny would happen. Pawlikowa's father had a stock of sugar to feed his bees in the winter and Pawlikowa would sometimes take some sugar. On Marysia noticing the "theft," her mother would plead, "Marysia please don't tell your grandfather that I took some sugar." But on one occasion Marysia was angry with her mother for some reason and complained to her grandfather at the first opportunity saying, "Grandfather, Mama took some of your sugar!"

On the first Christmas I spent at Pawlikowa's I dressed the Christmas tree together with Marysia and cooked cabbage. But I went to the Grzegorek couple to celebrate the festival. Rafał arrived from Jędrzejów and Heniek was with us too.

I moved with ease around the village and sometimes visited the homes of people I knew. However, I kept this to a minimum in order not to raise suspicion and because I didn't want to become too socially involved, especially with the boys.

The Nowak family lived near the Grzegorek's. They were an affluent family; they had had a store in Chlewice before the war. They had three children about my age: Stefan, Marysia, and Witek. All three of them had attended high school before the war in Włoszczowa, which was a rarity for children from a village such as Chlewice.

I befriended Marysia and whenever I visited the Grzegorek couple she would come also, as did Witek. Marysia confided in me her fondness for Mr. Stasio, i.e., Heniek. "You know Dzidka," she would say, "I like this Mr. Stasio a lot."

"I don't," was my curt reply.

In fact, Heniek was very likeable. He cut an impressive figure—was sharp and handsome, with chestnut hair, and dark eyes. On the other hand, Witek started to become somewhat infatuated with me and he confided in Heniek, whom he assumed was a stranger to me. Thus, both Heniek and I knew what was going on, which was important in order to be cautious in our personal relationships. But Witek kept pestering Heniek about me, saying, "Oh, this Dzidka! There is no other girl like her around here."

Heniek, or Mr. Stasio, tried to calm him down saying, "I don't know what you see in her. Look at her hair…"

Once a week, regular as clockwork, Rafał would come from Jędrzejów to visit us. Officially, he was my uncle from the Poznań region. Usually, we all met at the house of the Grzegorek couple and later, we would walk together to see him off. Usually, I asked some girl, usually Halina, to accompany me.

Before I arrived in Chlewice, Witek was courting a local girl, Hela. When he began looking in my direction, Hela was immediately notified. She turned jealous and began to dislike me. On one occasion the young people of Chlewice were gathered at someone's house. Witek and Hela were also present and they started having an argument in the presence of everyone there. One of the girls, who took Hela's side, wanted to put Witek on the hot spot, "Who are you so infatuated with? With a girl who has red hair, like a Jew?"

His reply was not long in coming, "You cannot hold a candle to her!" The fight continued.

For reasons like this all close social relationships could turn out to be dangerous for Heniek and myself, so I refused all kinds of invitations and meetings, excusing myself by saying that I had nothing to wear and I couldn't go out, which was actually true. I was also excused on the grounds of my grieving for my brother.

Heniek and I also had to be very, very careful in our relationship with each other—no intimacies or gestures of friendship. For me, he was some distant relative of the Grzegorek couple. Having been expelled from Wielkopolska, he somehow ended up with them and was staying for a while. I was Rafał's niece, who was believed to have known the Grzegorek couple as neighbors from the area where he had lived before the war.

I always addressed Heniek very officially, calling him "Mister," and he invariably addressed me as "Miss Dzidka." Thus, for example, whenever Marysia spoke to me about him, I made sure I kept the right form of address—Mr. Stasio, Mr. Stanisław or Mr. Staszek.

In Chlewice I got to know two brothers, also refugees from the Poznań region. One of them worked at the village administration office and addressed me as Miss Miecia, because of my name on the forged baptism certificate.

Following the example of other girls I started keeping a diary so that my acquaintances could inscribe their feelings for me. I always had it with me, carrying it from place to place. I don't remember anymore how it showed up or who gave it to me. Perhaps Rafał brought it to Chlewice. I kept it for many years after the war, but finally it got lost somewhere. Despite the loss, to this day I remember some poems and dedications inscribed inside.

Rafał wrote two little poems:

Heaven gave you the looks of the rose / But it was even more gracious to you / One can like a rose one day, but you are likeable forever.

And the second one:

You should be compared to a rose / With just one little difference / A rose is beautiful for a week / Whereas you are always the same.

Marysia Nowak wrote a well-known quote from the poet Adam Asnyk:

We were given the Koran and the Bible and each of these promises us happiness in our lethargic lives...

Someone else cited a poem by Adam Mickiewicz:

Have a heart and look into your heart...

And someone else wrote a simple poem:

I sit by a little table / Writing this in your diary / I write briefly and to the point / Because I love you, what do you have to say?

Witek Nowak, who courted me, wrote the following poem:

The noblest stone is the one / That cuts all others / And doesn't get hurt / The noblest heart is the one / Which prefers to be hurt / Than to hurt others.

Some poems were decorated with drawings of hearts, flowers, and such like.

Halina Grzegorek entered an interesting inscription. Deliberately and with full awareness she wrote a poem with patriotic overtones, which I always wanted to keep with me, because it provided a proof of sorts of my being Polish:

Even if your hands are bound with shackles / And tied to a wall in a quiet dungeon / Don't let your worries get the better of you / Don't give in to despair / Because you are a Polish girl, and Polish girls don't cry.

Others who inscribed something in my diary included Hanka Leszczyńska, Witek's former beau, Hela from Chlewice, as well as several other girls. Even though I had my diary with me throughout the occupation period, no inscriptions were entered after I left Chlewice.

Of course, I was asked about my family, what happened to them, etc. Bednarska asked me, as did Mr. and Mrs. Nowak and Pawlikowa. People were curious, but were also suspicious and mistrustful. On one occasion old Nowak aired his suspicions about me. He had an open mind, knew a lot, and had a lot of experience. He let me know that he suspected something, but chose not to follow up on it, by saying once, "Oh, this Dzidka has something about her. It is not clear where she is from or where she has she been."

Apart from the Grzegorek family, two brothers from the Poznań region, and us there were no other refugees in Chlewice. By expelling Poles to Generalgouvernement the Germans implemented the policy of scattering families, neighbors, and individuals to various places so that they wouldn't be together and would therefore feel more lonely and helpless in their new and strange surroundings.

The Germans deported the Jews of Chlewice to the Jędrzejów ghetto, and then all of the ghetto residents to Treblinka. The Germans allocated the evacuated Jewish houses to resettled locals and refugees. As it happened, the Grzegorek's were resettled in the house of the Fajgenblat family, our relatives from the side of Aunt Hendla from Jędrzejów, who had a bakery and in whose house we lived with my grandparents in the ghetto.

I discovered to my astonishment that the brother of Aunt Hendla's husband and his entire family were hiding in Chlewice. They had prepared in advance a hideout in one of the farms outside the village and hadn't gone to the ghetto. Instead, they had hidden there. The entire family—the parents with four grown-up children—survived the whole war hiding in that place, which was quite exceptional. After the war, they moved to Sosnowiec and then to Israel. One of them lives in Israel to this day. We knew about their existence from the Grzegorek couple, but they didn't know anything about Heniek or me.

Sometimes, at night, one of them went back to their house—where the Grzegorek couple was living and Heniek would disappear because he didn't want them to see him. It was safer this way for everyone. To the very end they didn't know about Heniek and me staying in Chlewice.

If someone had carefully prepared a good hideout and enjoyed good and trusting relationships with the farmers, the odds of survival were higher. But only a small number of Poles agreed to this arrangement and the rest of the Jews had only the anticipation of tragedy for their people. However, in some cases, Poles were not indifferent to the Jews and did not denounce them to the Germans.

A dramatic incident took place in Jędrzejów when a Jewish couple handed over their four-year-old son to a Polish family in order to hide him. The next day the family handed over the little boy to the Germans. People saw how the German, who led the boy to his execution, showed an uncharacteristic display of "kindness" by giving the boy some chocolate.

Often the hiding of Jews was denounced out of greed for the Jews' belongings as the denunciation would cover the act of looting. In other cases, Jews were denounced out of jealousy and antisemitic animosity.

A similar tragic end was met by the Miedziński family. They had lived outside Jędrzejów, on the same side of town as my grandparents, but a little closer, right behind the tracks, towards the monastery. They had several children; one of the girls was my age and had attended school with me. During the war, after the liquidation of the Jędrzejów ghetto, the Miedziński family was sheltered by a man named Mróz who received a lot of money and valuables for his trouble. Before the war the Miedzińskis were quite affluent because they had traded in grain.

Sometime later, probably in 1943, this man Mróz decided to kill the entire family, six persons, by asphyxiation. He sealed all the openings in the basement so that they couldn't breathe. Somehow they managed to break out and fled to the fields nearby. Then Mróz organized a posse of peasants who savagely murdered the entire family with long clubs. Mróz did this because he didn't want it to become known that he intended to finish off a Jewish family, which he had sheltered at his house. Local partisans quickly learned about this crime and on the second or third day they came to the Mróz's house and shot the entire family to death—Mróz, his wife, and their two small children. I learned of this story after the war, when I returned to Jędrzejów. Later, a trial took place in Kielce of all those who took part in the hunt and then mass murder of the Miedziński family.

Unfortunately, this wasn't the only case of its kind. Before the war Kielce was known for its antisemitism and anti-Jewish actions during the occupation. Not all the cases were solved. A man named Michał, for example, apparently took in some Jews and then killed them. A peasant family also offered a hideout to a Jewish family. It is not known what happened to them but none survived. In general, peasants did not have a good reputation as far as the treatment of Jews was concerned. I witnessed a great deal of aversion to Jews. The group most sympathetic to Jews was those who had resettled from Wielkopolska (Poznań).

At Pawlikowa's I felt pretty safe, even though unpleasant surprises awaited me from every possible direction. On one occasion Pawlikowa's father asked me suddenly, without any reason, "Did you see, Miss Dzidka, how they crush a glass during a Jewish wedding?"

"How could I know?" I replied. "I've never been to a Jewish wedding."

One day Mrs. Leszczyńska, acting the part of my aunt, came to visit me. Rafał had given me advance warning of her visit and I waited for her impatiently, and then dashed out with great joy to greet her. She wore an elegant black dress and a hat with a long mourning veil. Surprised, she said, "Dzidka, for heaven's sake! Look where you live, right by the road! This is terribly dangerous." It was true. In this place the risk of running accidentally into the Blue Police or Germans was much greater than if I lived on a side street. Also, I was much more visible here, provoking possible suspicion and

Sabina, 1945

conjectures. Aunt Leszczyńska, however, meant that someone from my area could recognize me, because Jędrzejów was not far away.

Shortly after this conversation, I left Pawlikowa's house. At that time, I didn't know whether Aunt Leszczyńska's opinion played a part in my decision or if other considerations were at play. In fact, it wasn't me at all who made decisions about my lodgings. It was Rafał, who had consulted Heniek and the Grzegorek couple. In January 1943, I left Pawlikowa's house and took up residence with Zofia Zającowa.

I discovered the reason for my moving out of Pawlikowa's house only 50 years later, when I found and visited her in the summer of 1997. It turns out that one day a young man, a teacher whom I had known a little while living in Chlewice, came to visit her. I was already asleep at the time so didn't hear the conversation, and later, no one told me what he had said. This is what I learned he had said to Pawlikowa: "Mrs. Pawlikowa, it's been confirmed, this Dzidka is Jewish. It is known where she is from and what's what. She must not be so rude and you must be careful."

It is not known whether he was speaking on behalf of someone else or how much he knew. In any event he spoke harshly, suggesting that this situation could end very badly for Pawlikowa. Perhaps he wanted to get back at me, because on one occasion I had been gruff when he showed some romantic interest in me.

Pawlikowa didn't say anything to me about this ill-boding visit, but she must have told the story to the Grzegorek couple, who in turn repeated the news to Rafał, which explains my move to another place. It is not clear why I remained in Chlewice, which for many reasons seemed "hot" and somewhat constricted, but everything was decided with haste and with few possibilities for maneuvering.

When I moved out of Pawlikowa's house, both of us cried because, despite the brief period of barely two months, we had grown used to each other. She liked me a lot and I, too, was fond of her.

Continuing my "journey," I couldn't feel safe anywhere. Anyone, anytime, could cast suspicion on me, which was liable to lead to my demise. Although I was of a Semitic type, I was protected by my demeanor and speech. I spoke pure Polish, without any accent, freely and spontaneously, which removed suspicions, but one could be exposed in a most stupid and banal fashion.

An incident—dramatic but also absurd in its stupidity—took place in Chlewice, of all places. One day, a brown-haired Polish girl from the neighboring village of Janowice was walking through the village. Suddenly, a peasant grabbed her by the hand and shouted, "Now you are mine, you Jewish hag!"

She started lamenting, "Let me go, I am from Janowice. We are neighbors. I live there with my family. Everyone there knows me." But it didn't help and this simpleton dragged her to his place and locked her in a little room. Things got sorted out even before he could report to the police that he had grabbed a Jew, as someone who recognized the girl came to him and the disappointed "hunter" had to let her go. I realized that something similar and completely unexpected could happen to me almost at any moment, anywhere. Except that, in such a case, no one would stand up for me. My saddest and most hopeless feelings were evoked by the disinterested hatred for the defenseless Jews and the cold satisfaction with our tragedy. I could understand when someone refused to help, even in cases of acquaintances who argued in their own defense that they couldn't, that they were afraid, that they could not take people in and give them shelter, and could only give us something to eat or to help financially. It was well known that helping Jews was punishable by death of the whole family. Under such circumstances it was difficult to hold a grudge, even though bitterness and sorrow remained. But if someone denounced a Jew, such villainy was hard to grasp. The open wound remained.

One example is Mr. Edek, an ex-military man, who turned out to be a monster. He was my girlfriend's uncle and had been a sergeant in the army. He didn't live in Jędrzejów before the war, but ended up there soon after the war began. During the war, shortly after the liquidation of the Jędrzejów ghetto, he hunted down a Jew in hiding and chased him like an animal. This Jew was captured in the field and brought by cart to Jędrzejów. Later, the Germans shot him to death. Even after the war this monstrous story was told in Jędrzejów.

During all my years of hiding, I encountered a great deal of primitive hatred of Jews. It was impossible to remain unnoticed; whenever a stranger showed up in the village, everyone knew about it within a short time and people's tongues immediately started wagging. At the utterance, "Dzidka was at Pawlikowa's," everyone knew about it immediately. People were suspicious, mistrustful, and greedy. It was very easy to arouse suspicion and people always talked about someone in hiding, or a Jew who was captured somewhere. They talked about it all the time; it was a staple of everyday conversation in houses, in the store, near the church, and I had to listen to them babbling and spreading rumors. Some people offered shelter, others talked about it, and still others denounced. I was fearful and lonely, being forced to show a happy face. My nerves were always taut and I was in the grip of fear almost all the time. Whenever I visited some family who didn't know my true identity, I had to be on guard at all times. As a 17-year-old girl in pain after the loss of all my loved ones, I couldn't afford to give the slightest excuse for suspicion. I wasn't quite certain what to say when people asked about my prewar whereabouts, about my family or my school. I was forced to listen to all kinds of stories, including those hostile to Jews, and to stupid anti-Jewish jokes, without ever being certain what they would say about me someday, whether someone would give me a strange look, utter an allusion or voice a suspicion. I didn't know how to behave when policemen or Germans showed up, and how others might behave, others for whom I—Dzidka from the Poznań region—was, after all, a stranger. Who would back me up? Who would help me? I was tense, fearful, and stressed all the time. In every new place I went to hide, wherever a place for me was allocated, I always had to know how to behave toward the new and strange people, which caused me more anxiety and fear.

At Zającowa's

At the end of January 1943, I started living at Zającowa's house. She was single, about 30 years old, and lived with her mother. Their house was located on the edge of Chlewice, on the Janowice side. From the front door, one entered a small hallway, which led to the living room where I had a bed in the corner.

Soon after I began living there, Witek Nowak started coming over; he wanted terribly to have a date with me and in order to avoid his courting I kept explaining that I had a fiancé who had stayed behind in the Poznań region. What could I do? This hiding behind a fictitious fiancé didn't look good and was liable to raise doubts, as people wondered how a young girl of 17 could already have a fiancé.

Rafał continued to visit me as my uncle and he looked askance at Witek, as he obviously didn't like his courting efforts. But he couldn't afford to react sharply, because, after all, he was just my uncle. Sometimes I laughed silently at his embarrassment.

The Zając woman was very gregarious and her girlfriends from the village visited her quite often. All of us sat together talking about everything. One day there were several of us—Zosia Zając, Marysia Nowak, some other girls, and I. A young man, tall and strong, was also there. During our conversation and horseplay, he grabbed me silently and put me on his knees, saying, "Well, we'll see how strong she is!"

I didn't like it at all, so I jumped off and replied sharply, "I won't stand for such jokes!"

"Just look at you, grand dame," he bristled.

"If you don't know how to behave, you should leave!" I burst out. His face turned red, he became ashamed of himself, and left. The girls were all flabbergasted by my behavior.

"Dzidka, he'll get back at you for this. You shouldn't have got into this. He is a tough, single man."

To which I replied, "What a brute! Look how he behaves. He thinks he can do as he likes."

I had my honor and dignity, but in that instance I got carried away by my temperament and hadn't paused to think whether I was doing the right thing or not. After all, he hadn't done anything terrible. I had reacted impulsively and had humiliated him in front of the other girls, which could turn against me. If only he had known who I really was…

One day, in the beginning of March, after I had been staying with the Zając woman for quite some time, the elder Zając woman returned home from the village and said to me, "Miss Dzidka, people in the village say that you are Jewish. Perhaps it would be better for you to move."

"Well, let them go and tell the Germans," I replied, trying to remain sanguine.

What else could I have said? Should I have said, "Yes, I am"? I couldn't do it. The Zając woman must have taken fright; after all, I was living in her house and if something happened to me, she and her daughter would also suffer the consequences. She warned me, but also let me understand that I needed to move out of her house.

I immediately went to the Grzegorek couple. I repeated to them the words and attitude of the old Zając woman. They unanimously concluded that I had to move out of there and that Chlewice was too "hot" for me to stay there any longer. However, they didn't want to rush things, because this would confirm the suspicions. Instead, they formulated a plan.

"Dzidka, go back to the Zając woman as if nothing has happened," they said. "In a little while, Halina will come to you and say that your parents were informed that your aunt has fallen ill and you must go to her because she's calling for you."

There was nothing to wait for, because the situation was getting more dangerous by the hour. All tense, I returned to the Zając home and waited for the alleged "news."

Later that day Halinka Grzegorek came to me and, in the presence of Zosia Zając, told me they had received news from my sick aunt, who, like me, was resettled from her native area, and was now living in Rakowo. Halinka said my aunt had been asking for me. Zosia didn't say anything and didn't even show any special reaction to my sudden departure. Quickly, I gathered my things, but I left behind my modest property—two dresses and some knick-knacks—as a guarantee of my return and in order to dispel any suspicions that I was in hiding and now was on the run again. This ruse was also designed to protect Heniek, who was staying at the Grzegorek couple's house. Although officially we had no connection and never lowered our guard, nonetheless, the discovery that I was hiding here as a resettled person would be enough to cause suspicion about other such persons in the village. I parted from Zosia Zając saying I would be away for a brief period and promised I would return.

I wondered why the Zając woman had begun to suspect that I was Jewish. There were many occasions and pretexts: Someone from Jędrzejów on a visit to Chlewice could have recognized me; or perhaps people had talked, made a link between various incidents, and begun sensing who I really was; someone could have begun to cast doubts over the real reasons behind my sojourn in Chlewice and wondered why I changed my address so often if I was a resettled person; or someone might have asked why "Uncle" Rafał and I didn't live together. So many times I had to explain what had happened to my hair and why it had a strange color. There was the story of my grieving for a brother, and finally, some unknown fiancé who didn't seem to have a permanent address. It was enough for someone to put everything together in order for a coherent tale to emerge. What did people from the village talk about in the evening in their cabins, near the church or in the store? Strangers were as good a topic as any for such conversations.

I stayed in Chlewice for several months, not in hiding, but living like a normal person among the other villagers. This was a sufficiently long enough period of time, with all the unfavorable circumstances that kept arising, to eventually make this place "hot" and dangerous.

After I left the Zając woman's home, I stopped by the Grzegorek couple's house. Witek Nowak had already learned about my departure and came to say goodbye. All he knew was that I was leaving to stay for a while with my sick aunt who lived in Rakowo. Together with Mrs. Grzegorek he escorted me a short distance from Chlewice, in the direction of Jędrzejów. Parting from me, he said that when I returned he'd let me in on a certain secret. It turned out his intentions towards me were very serious. Witek returned to Chlewice and we only met again 54 years later, in the summer of 1997.

AT LESZCZYŃSKI'S ONCE AGAIN

I left Chlewice, without the possibility of returning. We trudged slowly in the cold night. It was the end of February and the winter that year was very harsh. All I was wearing was thin shoes, a light dress, and a thin coat. I wore no stockings or sweater and I got terribly cold. We managed to reach Leszczyńska's house when it was still dark. Her house always served as a contact point for me and Heniek in these incessant wanderings, constantly hiding and escaping the fate that the Germans had in store for the Jews. I was still without any documents or papers, which got stuck in the village administration office, waiting for my *kenkarte* to be issued.

We could always count on Aunt Miecia's help. Mrs. Grzegorek told her what had happened and why I had had to leave Chlewice all of a sudden and for good. It was a decision taken by the Grzegorek couple on the fly. They did the right and proper thing.

After my departure from Chlewice we hatched a plot of sorts, as if against Rafał. As always in unexpected and difficult situations such as these, the first person to be notified was Rafał, who assumed the moral obligation to provide a hiding place and to take care of Heniek and me. Furthermore, he had bound himself to me emotionally and he desired and intended to marry me after the war. There was a huge age difference between us, and besides, in the situation I found myself in, I didn't make any plans for the future. I thought to myself that perhaps someone else could also help me and provide me with a hiding place, in order to avoid being bound to Rafał by any assumptions. Mrs. Grzegorek, who was privy to all aspects of this story, tried to persuade me to break my connection with him, and Aunt Leszczyńska also joined in, giving her own reasons. They trusted Rafał and were full of admiration for him, seeing his efforts, dedication, and determination, but they also had opinions of their own, which they laid out to me.

So, shortly before my departure from Chlewice, we decided to act without his involvement—the Grzegorek couple, Heniek, and I. We found ourselves in extraordinary and risky circumstances, in which a thin crack appeared. Mrs. Grzegorek gave me her advice and I agreed, as if without a will of my own. "Dzidka," she said, "you'll disappear and we'll tell him. You'll stay at Leszczyńska's for a while and later you'll move on. I'll take you to the Leszczyński's myself. We won't tell Rafał anything and later we'll think of something." And so it happened, that when we came to Aunt Miecia's house that night, Mrs. Grzegorek revealed her plan and Mrs. Leszczyńska agreed. I stayed with Mrs. Leszczyńska for the next few days.

As was his habit, Rafał arrived in Chlewice to visit me and see how things were going. The Grzegorek couple told him I wasn't there anymore, because some itinerant peddler had arrived in Chlewice from Częstochowa and had taken me with her. Meanwhile, I was actually staying at Leszczyńska's.

A few days later, Aunt Miecia set out for Chlewice to meet with the Grzegorek couple and Heniek to talk about what to do about me and where to direct their efforts, while Rafał still believed I was staying in Częstochowa. We decided that Aunt Miecia would also take with her a letter to Witek Nowak in which I would make excuses for my prolonged absence from the village. This letter was also meant to justify Aunt Miecia's arrival in Chlewice, where she was due to pick up some of the things I had left behind. We also hoped that her visit would nip in the bud all the rumors that spread after my departure about who I really was, and in this fashion Heniek would be indirectly protected too, because once woken, all the doubts and whispers needed a new place to rest, and strangers were the obvious target.

We composed the letter together—Maryla, Hania, and I. I wrote that, due to unexpected circumstances, my return to Chlewice would be delayed, because I had suddenly taken ill and was waiting for the removal of my appendix. I added a few generalities and sent Witek my greetings. Aunt Miecia went to Chlewice, but spent no more than two hours there; she spoke to Heniek and the Grzegorek couple, and passed on my letter to Witek.

Witek wrote back immediately and Aunt Miecia brought his reply to me, which in truth I hadn't expected. It turned out that Witek had been sincerely moved by my "illness," wished me a speedy recovery, assured me he would pray for me, and would even donate money towards a Holy Mass for me. Also, he expressed his deep feelings for me, that he was pained by our separation, and that after my return to Chlewice he wanted to ask me for my hand in marriage. He even mentioned that he had ordered a silver engagement ring for me. He conveyed his longing and nostalgia by paraphrasing two lines from a celebrated poem by a 16th century Polish poet, Jan Kochanowski. I didn't reply.

One week passed, then another, and Rafał kept going to the post office in the hope that he would receive a letter or just a few words letting him know where I was. He waited anxiously, tormenting himself.

Leszczyńska thought about sending me to Kraków because she had a cousin there, and she thought that perhaps I could stay with her until the end of the war. In Jędrzejów, she notified her friends Judge Szreniawski and his wife about my situation. I knew them from before the war and the judge's wife liked me a lot. They had been friends with my grandparents and truly wanted to help me. They sought various possibilities and thought that perhaps I could be sheltered by their relatives in Zagłębie. They discussed the matter with Aunt Miecia, but in truth it was very difficult to hide someone somewhere and then transport them and, in the end, the judge's wife said to me, "Well, my child, there is nothing I can do for you."

I was still living with Aunt Leszczyńska, but was prepared to leave at a moment's notice. I spent nights in various places—in the room, in the outhouse, in the attic, and one night even under a trough in the barn. One day, as I was hiding, I heard the peasants talking to each other. One asked, "Did anyone from the Mechel Landschaft family survive? They were such a decent family." On another occasion, I overheard a conversation between Aunt Miecia and Hela Piasecka, who had been resettled from Wielkopolska together with her parents and was living nearby. Heniek and I knew her from the occupation years. Hela was complaining while remembering us, "Such a pity about Heniek and Rózia, they were so young and pretty."

Aunt Leszczyńska answered her, smiling discreetly, "Why don't you pray for them, Hela, perhaps they will survive."

Rafał was still in the dark about me. He was convinced I was in Częstochawa and continued to wait for a letter or some news about me. Meanwhile, Mrs. Grzegorek arrived one day at the Leszczyński's house, saying that Heniek's situation in Chlewice had deteriorated. "Staszek, I mean

Heniek, has to be moved. After Dzidka's departure there was a buzz in the village. People began making links between facts and persons, and also there was talk that Staszek is a Jew. For the sake of everyone, his and ours, he has to be transferred from Chlewice."

The situation was getting worse by the day and the two women were still helpless. With our backs against the wall, overwhelmed by new complications and our inability to cope with them, we all decided to tell Rafał everything. It was decided jointly by Leszczyńska and Mrs. Grzegorek. Although my opinion didn't count for much, I felt the same. In order to clear up all this mess, the two women decided they would tell Rafał that I had just returned from Częstochowa, thus covering the entire plot, which, in fact, had been directed against Rafał.

While the three of us—Hania, Maryla, and I—stood watch by the window, someone went to bring Rafał to the house. Maryla, who was known for her sharp tongue and sense of humor, cried out suddenly, "Look, your Rafcio is flying, look how happy he is!"

Rafał came over and we greeted each other. He was beaming, while I felt embarrassed and ashamed because of this fracas, which he didn't know anything about. Leszczyńska and Mrs. Grzegorek told him about the events in Chlewice and Heniek's situation, and Rafał immediately set out in search of a new hideout. It wasn't easy for him, because he was a stranger in this area and didn't know the local residents. However, he remembered that his acquaintances from Wielkopolska, or perhaps some former students of his from the time he spent in the Generalgouvernement, lived nearby. In the first period after the expulsions, Rafał had lived in the Miechów area, where he taught for a short time in the Koszyce local trade school. He remembered that a former student now worked as a ferryman in a little village on the Vistula River, about 20 kilometers from Kazimierz. He set out thinking that this would be the safest place for me.

While we waited hopefully at Mrs. Leszczyńska's for his return, we endured a dramatic Nazi manhunt. The Germans usually came before dawn and I told Aunt Miecia that if they ever came looking, she should wake me up so that I could go to some empty space and they could grab me without involving her and her family. This is what Aunt Miecia did, even though her servant was opposed to this, asking, "Why did you wake her up?" I was hidden under the cow trough, which he thought was a safe place. The Germans, however, brought dogs so the risk was considerable. Maryla and Hania took flight, as did the other young people, but I couldn't join them. I came out from under the trough and stood by the side of the road, covered in a shawl. At some point Władek Maludziński walked up to me, lifted my shawl and said, "Tola, go home. The Germans have left." He pretended, of course, not to recognize me. Later, Jula Taborek also came to me, and, just like Władek, pretended she didn't know me, because her sister Krysia was standing nearby asking about me. Jula replied, "This is a girl servant of the judges Szreniawski." However, news spread about me being spotted and because this took place on the grounds of the estate, it wasn't difficult to figure out where I was actually staying. In the afternoon, when Hania went to visit some acquaintances of hers, they asked her who had been standing in the field. After Hania returned with the news, poor Auntie suffered a nervous breakdown—she was literally trembling.

Rafał found his former student and asked him for help, saying that he would bring his fiancée to him for a spell. I was no longer his niece, as he had presented me until then, but his fiancée. The day of my departure arrived and I was making preparations for the journey. We were to travel by a narrow-gauge train. Everything, it seemed, was going well.

Aunt Leszczyńska's old father, Płatkowski, lived with her. He was a brave old man, full of energy. Every evening, we faced the same problem: Where I would spend the night and where should I go in case of danger? On German orders, people covered their windows at night with black paper. Once, Płatkowski, full of bravado, said, "Goddamnit, if the Germans come, let Dzidka hide behind this black paper. Płatkowski was always curious about what happened in the house and asked about everything. Once, he was sitting with Rafał in the drawing room. They were alone. Aunt Miecia had just left and I was someplace else. Grandfather Płatkowski started asking questions, "So, where are you taking her?"

"We are going someplace else," Rafał replied evasively.

Of course he didn't want to tell him where we were going, so that later Grandfather wouldn't shoot off his mouth. Płatkowski repeated his question, but Rafał refused to tell him. The old man was disappointed and irritated that secrets were being kept from him, and he angrily replied to Rafał.

"Aha, so you don't want to tell me where you're taking her. But you must know that for the past two weeks she was hiding here, and you knew nothing about it!"

Astonished, Rafał replied angrily, "Oh, you are all phonies. I run to the post office like crazy, I am looking for a letter, and meanwhile you were in Częstochowa, right?! You are a phony just like the rest. It was always like that, 'When in trouble, run to the Jew,' but now it's changed, 'When in trouble, run to Rafał. Arrange this for that person, help, and then, just go.' You are impostors, all of you!"

He ran out of the mansion and kept screaming in the farmyard, without seeing me. I was hidden and kept quiet, listening to all this commotion and wondering what had happened there, had everyone gone crazy?

Troubled by all the yelling, Mrs. Leszczyńska came over and listened to Rafał, who angrily told her why he was shouting and what he thought about all that. Aunt Miecia reproached her father, "Daddy, what have you done?"

"Goddammit," he replied. "When Kałowski didn't want to tell me where he was taking her, I got back at him and told him that she had been here all that time while he didn't know anything."

The situation was tense, but we had to go. Rafał did not renege on his promise. We left the house. In the evening after dark, we reached the railway station in Jędrzejów, which was located on the outskirts of town. We traveled by narrow-gauge railway, in a private car, to Kazimierza Wielka. Rafał kept reproaching me all the time, "Had I known earlier about all this, I would have just spat on it and stopped bothering with it."

He kept on with his anger, but there was nothing to be done. He didn't go back on the promise he made to us and to himself. Someone else might really have left me alone, stopped taking risks, washed his hands of the whole business, and turned his back on me. But Rafał persisted courageously despite all kinds of obstacles and difficulties, which kept besetting him, even from the least expected direction.

It was March. What was my situation? Jędrzejów had become a "hot" place for me, as had Chlewice. I was still without documents, while relations with Rafał had become very tense. Heniek was also in great danger. I was traveling into the unknown, starting everything afresh for the umpteenth time. I had no idea what was awaiting me. I was very depressed and dispirited.

IN DĄBRÓWKA MORSKA

Upon reaching Kazimierza Wielka, we walked about 20 kilometers and reached the Vistula River. A boat steered by the boatman carried us across the river to the south bank to a little village called Dąbrówka Morska. By the time we reached the house and the end of our journey, we were very tired. The little house was situated very low, as if at the foot of the embankment, and the river flowed right behind it. At the shore a ferryboat was tied. The ferryman, Tadeusz, Rafał's former student, lived together with his mother and younger sister Emilia, Miss Mila, who was slightly older than me, about 20.

We greeted each other. They were expecting our arrival. Rafał introduced me as his fiancée. He said he wanted to leave me with them for a spell, because he would be away on unspecified business. He did not expect me to stay there for long, because this place was not suitable for a long-term safe hideout, but once he learned that Chlewice was "hot," he didn't have enough time to arrange anything else.

I didn't know where he came up with the idea of me being his fiancée. From the very beginning, this guise was unclear and suspect. Later, Rafał realized it was a mistake. In the evening, when it was almost time to go to bed, the landlord prepared separate rooms for us. The residents, Rafał, and I were in the kitchen at the time.

At some point, I called Miss Emilia outside and in the hallway I asked her to sleep with me in the same room, to which she agreed. I didn't take into account that this arrangement would be improperly understood by the owners. In the morning, Rafał was very upset, reproaching me for putting him in an awkward situation, which aroused suspicion on the part of our hosts. I didn't try to explain my behavior or say sorry to him, because at that time I didn't understand that I was behaving imprudently.

Still angry, Rafał departed for Chlewice to take Heniek with him, because that hiding place was already burning under his feet. Rafał took Heniek surreptitiously back to the Leszczyński's mansion where he left him and right away set out again for Dąbrówka Morska. Meanwhile, the atmosphere in the fishing village was getting unpleasant. They began making jokes at Rafał's expense, saying, "What kind of fiancé is this? He could be Miss Dzidka's father." I wasn't good at playing games and was not overly familiar with the human psyche, so I started laughing with them. It seems that they suspected the charade very quickly, already on the second day.

Without warning, Tadeusz, the young ferryman, placed a page torn from a Jewish prayer book in front of me and provocatively asked, "Perhaps Miss Dzidka could read it for me?"

"And how I am supposed to know what it is?" I replied.

It goes without saying that I knew what he was after. I knew what they were thinking. However, in general, they behaved properly and did not broach this topic again. When someone stopped by for a visit and we started talking, as is usually the case, about everything and nothing, my hosts took care to discuss subjects that did not arouse suspicions.

Days passed, a week. I was having a difficult time there. Finally, Rafał arrived and brought me a letter from Heniek. Rafał had spent time at Heniek's place, spoke with him, and told him about the recent events and unpleasant situations he found himself in because of me. He complained to Heniek, and recounted the story of the intrigue which Mrs. Grzegorek, Aunt Leszczyńska, and I had hatched against him. He also complained to my uncle that "Miss Rózia" didn't have feelings for him; on the contrary, she mistrusted him.

Heniek cried while writing his letter to me—Mrs. Grzegorek later told me about it. He stressed that Rafał had been strongly affected by recent events, and remained dispirited and full of doubts whether he should continue with his risky efforts to hide us. Furthermore, as a Polish officer, Rafał could ill afford to feel safe: The Germans had officer registries and after manhunts, dragnets, roundups, and arrests, they checked the lists to see whether someone had fallen into their hands. Such persons were often victims of Nazi reprisals or were taken hostage. In view of this, Rafał had to be careful at all times; he had not always slept at home when he lived in Skroniów, later at my grandparents' house, and especially when he was on the road while taking care of Heniek and me.

In his letter, Heniek told me that only Rafał could save us and we could rely only on him, as we could see for ourselves from numerous instances. He also made it crystal clear, "You must know that only he can save us."

This was a very difficult meeting for Heniek and Rafał; at the same time, it was also decisive for our future fortunes. Rafał confirmed that he wanted to save us and promised that he would do so at any price. This was his word of honor, which he regarded as sacred.

I remember, when we were still in the ghetto and Rafał promised my grandparents he would do everything to save me, other young people also asked him to take care of them. In the small ghetto, one of our cousins had opened her closet, intending to offer him everything if he could smuggle her out of the ghetto and hide her (luckily she survived), but Rafał would not make false promises and refused, saying he had already made a promise to save me.

I finished reading Heniek's letter. I was very young then, I looked at everything differently, and didn't make any plans for the future. Also, I didn't have any special feelings for Rafał, and he knew it.

This was a very difficult moment, as I faced all the problems without a way out and without hope. Full of despair, I was in a blind alley. I was ready to commit suicide in the Vistula River. I even made it as far as the other side of the anti-flood embankment and was walking towards the water. Rafał, who had left the cabin a short while before and was searching for me, saw what was happening and ran after me. "What are you doing?!" he shouted. We turned back and sat next to each other. He related to me what he was told by our hosts: "We know what's going on. Why are you bothering with this, what do you need this Jew for? She is just a Jew and on top of it, she makes fun of you. You can't leave her here. Take her from here and bring her back to the place you took her from. What's the matter, there are not enough Polish women?"

He, too, went through very difficult moments. "It's over. They know everything," he said quietly, his voice barely a whisper. "What should I do now?" He addressed this question to himself.

"What shall we do?" I asked, feeling completely helpless.

"Get dressed. We are getting the hell out of here."

"Where, where to now? I can't do this anymore," I said, overcome by despair. "It's all the same to me. Let this life end already, because I can't go on like this."

We sat on top of the embankment looking at the flowing Vistula. Rafał was depressed and dejected. He started talking to himself, "What now? Everything is out in the open. Heniek has to be taken away from there. What should I do?"

Indeed, he was like a trapped animal. He did everything disinterestedly. He sold the things he owned, worked to save us, and provide our upkeep. I had left the ghetto with just the clothes I was wearing. Heniek had several sets of clothing and a small amount of money. Rafał paid for everything, especially the rent of our lodgings. Meanwhile, the situation was getting more and more complicated. It was as if everything had turned against him, and it was getting increasingly difficult.

When he had traveled back to Dąbrówka Morska to visit me and see my surroundings for himself, he didn't know that I would have to leave, that my time there was over. He had wanted to show himself to the hosts, bring a letter from Heniek, and was due to go back to Chlewice in order to move Heniek to a new place of hiding. Meanwhile, the events unfolded in a different direction, placing Rafał again in a position where he faced new obstacles and problems.

In his letter to me, Heniek said that his situation was very difficult and that only Rafał could save him, by moving him to another place. But in the meantime, Rafał and I found ourselves in a critical situation. We kept sitting on the embankment and Rafał began recalling his various acquaintances and places where he could hide me. He knew that acquaintances of his, by the name of Wieczorek, lived in the village of Słomka, near Bochnia. He decided that we would go there. To do so, we had to travel a distance of about 30 kilometers.

IN SŁOMKA

Rafał decided that we should leave immediately. While walking, I summoned up the courage and said to him, "Please, don't tell people that I am your fiancée. People have eyes and know what's what. Right away they know that something is wrong." He agreed with me.

Evening fell. We kept on walking all through the night, barely resting. I was cold, tired, and hungry when finally, towards morning, we arrived at the Wieczoreks' house in Słomka. The village was situated about seven, perhaps eight kilometers from Bochnia.

Rafał introduced me to his hosts as his niece. The Wieczorek couple, Nepomucen, Marta, and their two sons, had also been resettled from the Poznań region by the Germans. Rafał knew them well from before the war. He was a school principal and knew many people who respected him and held him in high regard. This was the reason why so many houses were open to him during these difficult years of the occupation. Despite being scattered in many localities, the Wielkopolska natives found each other, helped each other, and supported each other in times of trouble.

The Wieczorek couple welcomed us with open arms and immediately served breakfast, which I would remember for a long time. There were crack-lings made of pork fat and I gobbled up a huge quantity of them because I was starving. Immediately, I felt sick: First, pork didn't agree with me; second, I wasn't accustomed to fatty foods; and, third, I swallowed all of it on an empty stomach. Wieczorek gave me vodka with pepper to drink, a medicine recom-mended by his wife. Despite this, I suffered from stomachache for the next few days.

In this fashion, quite unexpectedly, began my sojourn at the Wieczorek couple's house in Słomka. Rafał left me there and went back to get Heniek. The Wieczorek couple and their two sons, Władek and Tadek, lived in a small house, with two rooms. Also, another person lived with them, a former student from Vilno, who helped Wieczorek with his labors. Wieczorek was involved in illegal slaughter, buying pigs from other farmers, making pork products, and then selling them. They lived from these illicit dealings, with the constant risk of being exposed by the Germans or Blue Police, or the fear of denunciation. The dealings themselves were very risky; it was easy to stumble, not to mention the fact that these activities were punishable by death.

Rafał did not tarry in Słomka and immediately returned to Jędrzejów to bring Heniek, who was staying with Aunt Leszczyńska. He spent only two days and two nights there. During his sojourn there, some partisans came to the house of Gorczak, a German informant, who was living with his wife and daughter in an apartment located in the school building. Gorczak, who was drunk, refused to open the door, so the partisans broke the door open. Gorczak's wife jumped out of the window. The partisans shot Gorczak right then and there, but didn't do anything to his wife or daughter. Later, people expected reprisals on the part of the Germans and the situation became very dangerous. Most afraid was Hania Leszczyńska, who kept asking Rafał, who showed up the next day, "When will you take Heniek? When?"

In the evening, Rafał took Heniek with him on a train in the direction of Kraków. Aunt Miecia and Władek Felis, a servant and confidante of the

Leszczyńskis, who was in on the secret, took Heniek to the railroad station in a cart, covered with straw.

The route passed from Jędrzejów to Kraków, and then from Bochnia to Słomka. There was a considerable commotion at the Kraków railroad station. Germans were asking for papers and conducting searches. They were looking for tobacco, meat, and pork fat, because that's what people dealt and traded in, supplying food to the large urban population that was suffering the most from hunger.

At that time Heniek, like me, didn't have any papers, i.e., a *kenkarte*, because he hadn't had enough time to secure it in Chlewice. Rafał was with him at all times so that he could somehow protect him or defend him in case of danger. Both of them kept moving around the train station to avoid the Germans; when the gendarmes gathered on one side, they moved to another. Heniek felt that danger was increasing and tried to talk Rafał into getting away to avoid capture. But Rafał refused and kept Heniek close to him. Somehow they managed to emerge unscathed from this situation, traveled by train to Bochnia, and from there they went by foot to Słomka where I was anxiously waiting for them. We were together again. Rafał introduced Heniek as his cousin. The three of us took up lodgings, not at the Wieczorek's, but in a room that Rafał had rented from some woman in a house nearby.

When we arrived in Słomka, I had no dress apart from the one I wore and two blouses that I had received from Maryla Leszczyńska. I had left the rest of my belongings in Chlewice, at the Zając woman's house, to disguise my real reason for leaving Chlewice, and later events unfolded so fast and so dramatically that there had been no time or occasion to think about my clothes. Only in Słomka did we have a moment of rest—very brief, as it turned out—to think about some clothes.

The main ghetto in Bochnia had been liquidated too, but, as we learned, the Germans had left in place a group of Jews who carried foreign passports—American or Canadian. These Jews did not live within the former ghetto, but in town, under supervision, though they were granted minimal freedom. They were still around, still alive, until the end, refusing to see the fate that the Germans had prepared for them. The Germans left them, perhaps, to lay hands on all of their property and money, which they thought was hidden.

Rafał proposed, or rather decided, that we would go to Bochnia, to these "foreign" Jews, to buy from them some clothes for me. He took me to a family whose address someone had given him. We entered and Rafał asked, "Can you guess who this young woman is?"

"No," they replied.

"She is Jewish," he said.

"And why are you telling us this?" they asked.

"Because I am talking to her people," he replied.

"You must not do it again. There are informants here. You must be more careful," they said.

We bought a shirt, a dress, a skirt, and a blouse. We abided by their warnings and made our way back through fields, bypassing Bochnia. Shortly after our departure, a man came to them. He had been standing nearby in civilian clothes, watching Jewish houses, and started asking them who we were, where we went, and what they knew about the young Jew he recognized me to be. They replied that they didn't know who we were or where we had come from. He warned them that they could be arrested and punished for maintaining such contacts.

We went there on a second occasion to get some more clothes and then they told us about the police informant, warning Rafał not to show up there with me anymore. Rafał replied with bravado, "If he had run into us, I would have broken his neck." But we didn't go there anymore.

Those Jewish foreign passport owners didn't know what awaited them. They didn't believe the worst, even though the extermination of thousands of Jews and the liquidation of ghettos was already known. They deluded themselves, or were simply convinced, that they were in a different, "better" situation, and that a foreign passport protected them and offered them security. They had both the opportunity and possibility to escape, but they stayed put in Bochnia, trusting in their safety, believing that nothing bad would happen to them, and so they waited for the promised journey to freedom.

In fact, one day, the Germans brought a passenger train, inviting everyone into the elegant passenger—not cattle—cars. Thus, they traveled first class to the extermination and concentration camps. They were convinced to the end that they were being transported abroad, in accordance with German promises. They trusted their passports and the "civilized culture" of the Germans.

Today, people speak about it differently, often expressing astonishment that everyone went like a sheep to slaughter. But at that time, no one could realize the magnitude of the German aggressor's savagery. There was no precedent in human history that could prepare us for this course of events. In the Jędrzejów ghetto, when adults talked sometimes about the possible resettlement, they thought that, although it was not clear what fate would meet older people, they were convinced that the young would be transported somewhere for forced labor, somewhere in the Polesie region perhaps, to drain swamps.

These were the rumors and conjectures that made the rounds then. No one had any idea or imagination to realize what fate the Germans planned for the Jewish people. It is possible that many tried to escape or do something to save themselves. Despite this ignorance, a kind of ill-boding hung over the conversations and in people's hearts.

This is why, when Rafał visited us in the ghetto, Grandmother kept repeating and reminding him of her request, that the moment he learned about any danger, he would immediately come over and take me with him. Grandfather and Heniek also requested this of him. I was sitting quietly, feeling that I wasn't in a position to ask for anything. Perhaps they sensed the fate awaiting the Jews, more by instinct than by reason. I often heard the echo of this in my father's statements.

However, there was no explicit talk about extermination. Everybody knew that things were not good. Everybody knew that the situation they found themselves in was unprecedented; even very old people had not experienced anything like this in their long lives. Nothing was known about concentration camps. For their part, the Germans did everything they could to shroud everything in mystery and ruses. They carried out the exterminations according to a well thought-out plan, one after another. All communications were down; we didn't know, for example, what was happening in Kraków. I didn't know about the ghetto in Bochnia, where I went later to buy clothes. No one in Bochnia knew what had happened in Jędrzejów.

It wasn't very often that someone tried to preempt German actions, and even then it was usually fruitless. My cousins, the Belfers, removed their small child from the ghetto and took him to their relatives in some little town in the hope that he would be safe there. They had waited for his birth for 16 years! Nothing doing. The Germans liquidated the ghetto in this town even before the liquidation of the ghetto in Jędrzejów. Their beloved child died together with others, far from his parents.

Perhaps underground organizations in large cities knew more about the fate of the Jews, but in 1942 these organizations were not yet developed, especially in the area of exchange of information and coordination of activities. And, years later, it emerged that, even if information about the extermination of Jews had trickled in, people disbelieved it, because it was beyond human imagination. Even Rafał, being on the move all the time, meeting many people, including the underground circles, didn't have much reliable information about the terrible events that were taking place so close and parallel to our vicissitudes.

It was May 1943. We would go with Heniek to church, as others did, for May masses. The church was small and made of wood, a typical countryside church. We couldn't afford to be absent, because this would arouse someone's suspicions. Heniek knew how to behave in general, even though I was better informed.

Problems refused to leave us. Sometime later, Mrs. Grzegorek came to see us. The Grzegorek couple planned to leave Chlewice—their situation in the village had taken a turn for the worse. They were aware of our whereabouts, which was why Mrs. Grzegorek arrived in Słomka to look for a new place for her family.

She spent several days with us, checking out Słomka and the neighboring villages. She found an apartment for rent in Jodłówka, a village located seven kilometers east of Bochnia, next to the railway line. She discovered that Witold Sakowski, a bachelor about 25 years old, was living there; he knew Rafał and the Wieczorek and Grzegorek families from Grodziec. Together with him lived two cousins, a mother and her daughter (whom he married after the war). Sakowski was involved in the production of illegal liquor, called *bimber,* and Heniek went to him to try to make a few pennies. All that Sakowski knew about Heniek was that his name was Julek, and that he was Rafał's cousin.

After the arrival of Heniek and Mrs. Grzegorek, the woman at whose place we lived began nursing suspicions that an entire Jewish family had arrived in the village and taken up lodgings with her. Mrs. Grzegorek, a Wielkopolska native, had features more Jewish than Heniek's or mine. Rafał also had a somewhat "Semitic" look.

The "healthy," creeping antisemitism refused to die. The woman whose room Rafał had rented for us started making noises and gossiping, saying that Jews had come to live with her. Thus, right from the beginning, our new place of residence became "hot."

We had to act quickly, but we couldn't move out again. In view of this, Rafał rented a room for himself and Heniek in a former Jewish house on the other side of the village. The house stood by the road to Bochnia. Mrs. Grzegorek quickly left. I vanished and went into hiding.

A new period in my life began. I had to remain in hiding and didn't show my face in the village. A cubbyhole was attached to the house and I slept there. The situation seemed to have calmed down. Rafał left the school in Skroniów and Jędrzejów and stayed with us. He traveled to Kraków to buy saccharine, which he later sold so that we could live on something. He traveled throughout the area in search of a new place for me. He went south, beyond Bochnia, in the direction of Wiśnicz, in the foothills of the mountains.

It was end of May 1943. I was still living in Słomka without the neighbors' knowledge. In the other part of the house in which we had rented the room lived a married couple. We had a separate entrance from the backyard, but even then we had to be very careful to remain out of their sight. During the day I was usually locked in the room where Rafał and Heniek slept. At night I moved to the cubbyhole in the backyard. Many times I was seized by fear.

One day, for example, evening came but I was still alone. Rafał had gone to Kraków and wasn't back yet. Despite the late hour, Heniek, who worked for Wieczorek, had not returned. I could neither leave nor move, and I was getting cold, because the nights were still chilly. I was riddled with worry that perhaps Rafał had been captured or Heniek had "got burned" at Wieczorek's. I was afraid that the Germans would come for me at any moment. I couldn't fall asleep, exhausted as I was from looking out of the window, awaiting Heniek's return.

This particular room was not safe: It it stood right next to the road, which was often used by the Germans. They could stop by or someone else could appear, just out of curiosity. The real danger was napping. In case of a visit by a patrol, Rafał and Heniek were prepared to escape through the window, on the backyard side. They had to be alert at all times, which is why one of them always kept watch, on the lookout for danger ahead. Rafał was very conscientious about his watchman duty, and he spent the time wrapped in the fur coat, which he had taken with him during resettlement from Grodziec and which accompanied him in the years of his wanderings. When it was Heniek's turn, he usually tried to talk himself out of it, saying that nothing unexpected or dangerous could happen that night. In line with this, he always changed into pajamas.

One night, Rafał noticed something dangerous—an automobile stopped nearby—and immediately woke up Heniek. Heniek jumped out of bed and started looking feverishly for his shoes in the darkness, asking Rafał where they could be. Rafał answered jocularly, "Now, go ahead and escape in pajamas. When I said that something could happen, you didn't listen to me, because you thought that today nothing would happen." Fortunately, it turned out to be a false alarm, but for Heniek it served as a lesson in prudence.

The Wieczorek couple didn't know I was living in Słomka. They thought I had just passed through the village and left together with Mrs. Grzegorek, who came for me. All they knew about Julek, i.e., Heniek, was that he was Rafał's cousin. It was enough for them, because they trusted Rafał.

Sometimes Heniek returned from the Wieczorek's very late as he would sit with them for a long time after work. He couldn't say he was in a hurry to get home, because they would have immediately started asking him why and suspicions would immediately surface. Sometimes they would work late into the night at slaughtering or meat preparation and then Heniek didn't return at all, spending the night with the Wieczorek couple. He couldn't always give me advance warning, especially when Rafał wasn't around, and even he was not always able to check with Heniek, whereas I stayed where I was, full of anxiety. A fear would seize me, while my imagination kept suggesting the worst scenario: Germans had raided the Wieczorek's house, they had discovered the clandestine slaughter of livestock, they had taken Heniek with them, and he would be gone for good. I was also suffering physically, being locked up in my cubbyhole, hungry and lonely. I cried and tormented myself. There was nothing I could do. I waited for them as one waits for compassion. I would fall asleep very tired, in torments that led to apathy: Come what may, it's all the same to me. Many times I went through difficult nights in Słomka, despairing and anxious.

Rafał kept looking for another place for me, a place where I wouldn't have to hide all the time, not only because he saw how difficult the current arrangement was for me, but also because it wasn't very good as far as either Heniek's or Rafał's safety was concerned.

Days passed. Meanwhile, in July, the Grzegorek family, who had left Chlewice, arrived in Jodłówka. They settled in a rented house in the village.

Rafał thought that perhaps I would feel better there. He moved me to their house, but I only stayed for two days. The Grzegorek couple clearly didn't want me to live with them. Out of carelessness, or perhaps deliberately, they exposed my identity to Sakowski's cousin, which turned Jodłówka into a "hot" place for me.

I returned to my cubbyhole in Słomka. The Grzegorek couple spent the rest of the war in Jodłówka.

IN ŁĄKTA GÓRNA

South of Bochnia and Nowy Wiśnicz, two villages nestled next to each other in a piedmont: Łąkta Górna and Łąkta Dolna. Rafał had lived there for some time immediately after his expulsion from Grodziec by the Germans. In Łąkta Górna there still lived Rafał's remaining acquaintances, who had also been resettled from their area, Turek, in Kalisz County. One was the Tarczyński family with three children, who knew Rafał from before the war because Tarczyński worked as a manager in the estate nearby. Rafał went to them to arrange a new place of hiding and living for me. They agreed to take me in.

We set out for Łąkta Górna. We had to walk about 20 kilometers, crossing Bochnia and Nowy Wiśnicz. We walked during the day. At some point, when we were passing through Bochnia, Rafał said suddenly, "It's important that we pass by this building." The building in question housed the headquarters of a German gendarmerie. Just then, as if summoned, several German gendarmes came out and started walking toward us. We couldn't retreat or turn away, because this would certainly have made them notice us. Rafał told me to walk slightly behind him, and in this fashion we passed them by, tense and fearful. They didn't stop us.

We reached Łąkta Górna. Rafał introduced me as his niece and immediately returned to Słomka. The Tarczyński couple, Tadeusz and Zosia, had three boys, the youngest of whom was born during the war. Their names were Janek, Rysio, and Józio. Everyone in this foothill village was poor, but it was especially hard for the resettled people, because they had no field to till, no farmyard, not even a cow.

We ate the same dish in the morning, at noon, and in the evening: a watery, sour soup and some potatoes in their skins. The soup, which stood on the windowsill, tasted like brackish water. We kept eating these potatoes, washing them down with the "soup." There was no bread at all. Sometimes, when the family managed to get their hands on a handful of flour, the lady of the house would make dough and then we baked pancakes on the kitchen hot plate. For drinking, there was a brew made from lime-tree flowers. It was in Łąkta Górna that I suffered from hunger most.

There were no beds, just straw pallets on the clay floor. Mr. Tarczyński worked intermittently, grabbing any job that came his way. But work was very hard to come by both in Łąkta Górna and in the neighboring villages. Farm owners had their sons or neighbors and helped each other. Strangers were treated with wariness. The Tarczyńskis kept selling their clothes, which they had brought with them from the Poznań region, to get some money for food to survive for a while longer. They also had some money from Rafał, who paid them for my upkeep. Their children were sickly and sad. The youngest, Józio, liked me a lot and addressed me as "auntie." He kept asking me to tell him about cookies, candy, and the Mother of God.

Rafał and Heniek would visit once a week, usually on a Saturday or Sunday. Sometimes they brought a little food with them. Sometimes just Rafał came. The roles were now reversed, with Heniek playing the part of my fiancé. He was six years older than I was and this "engagement" of ours was plausible enough not to give rise to gossip. When a local boy—a *chodak*, as they were called in the village—wanted to court me, I had my excuse ready to refuse meetings with him.

On one occasion, when Rafał and Heniek came for a visit, the Tarczyńska woman said with admiration, "Dzidka, you'll make a wonderful couple, you are so very much like each other." She meant Heniek and I, whom she regarded as a perfect match.

The Tarczyńskis' children were also hungry. One of the boys had a heart problem. Someone in the village said that blueberries were good for this kind of ailment, so we would climb to the nearby forest and gather blueberries for him. We also gathered lime-tree flowers to brew our "tea." There was no milk for the children; only now and then did Mrs. Tarczyńska manage to get or buy some from a local woman.

Summer passed, July and August 1943. During my stay in Łąkta Górna, Rafał resumed his efforts to get me a *kenkarte*. First, he had a new baptism certificate made for me, since the previous one had been left behind in Chlewice, and under the prevailing circumstances it would have seemed very suspicious to withdraw my papers from the village administration. Besides, Rafał couldn't show his face in Chlewice again. In any event, the new certificate was issued for Wiesława Królikowska and was forged, of course. We submitted the document, together with three fingerprints, to the village administration office in Trzciana. Again, we settled in for a long wait.

After some time—a month, perhaps longer—Rafał and I went to the village administration office to find out whether my *kenkarte* was ready for me. We waited in front of the building. Next to us stood several Blue Policemen who started looking at me. Something was not to their liking, because one of them signaled with his hand and called, "Come over here, little girl." There was nothing I could do. I started walking in their direction, but luckily Rafał noticed what was going on and walked up to them first, saying, "Greetings. Dzidka, introduce yourself to these gentlemen." They knew him because they remembered him from his sojourn in Łąkta Górna, right after the resettlement. "This is my niece," he told them. "In that case," they said, "it's nice to see you." They changed their tune immediately and began joking with us. Had Rafał not covered for me, they would have started asking questions, demanding to see my papers, applying pressure, and my fate would have been rather different.

During my stay in Łąkta Górna, Rafał went to nearby Rabka where his brother Adam, a musician, lived with his wife and children. He had bought a lot there before the war but didn't have time to build a house there, and resided elsewhere in Rabka. Adam's wife was fluent in German and worked in forest administration. However, Rafał couldn't place me with them, because this would have been dangerous in his opinion, both for me (there were a lot of Germans in Rabka) and for Adam's family.

The *kenkarte* business dragged on. Despite my long sojourn in Łąkta at the Tarczyńskis, we couldn't make things move along at the village administration office in Trzciana before I left. I was still without any official documents which, of course, increased the risk involved in hiding among people and moving from one location to another. Time and again I would find myself in dangerous situations. I had to be alert and be cautious with others. I went through "adventures" all the time.

Not far from our place lived Wisia, a dressmaker, resettled from Wielkopolska. We became close and I visited her often. One day I was returning from visiting Wisia. Just as I was coming out of the path that led to the house on the main road, I looked and got chills: In front of the house where I lived stood some Germans and a horse cart. They were talking among themselves, perhaps asking for something. I turned around quickly. They noticed me and started calling out to me to come to them. The distance between us wasn't great. I didn't flee, but started walking in the opposite direction. I passed by Wisia's house and turned into the backyard. I started running, knowing that the Germans couldn't see me anymore. I didn't know whether they were pursuing me or just calling out.

Exactly at that moment Mrs. Wisia was standing at the window and saw my unexpected return and me running. She called out to me, "Miss Dzidka, what happened? Where are you going?" I didn't answer, just crossed the backyard and went behind the house. There, as was usually the case in such places, stood the outhouse. I burst inside and latched the door. I didn't look back once to see whether the German soldiers were following me, but I sensed that this was the case. Right away I thought that they had come for me, to the place where I lived, and I just happened to arrive at that particular moment. I was terrified to the point of numbness. My whole life passed in front of my eyes as if in a kaleidoscope: various images, events, faces, and colors; shock, fear, and then a strange calm, a kind of apathy. I was standing inside, in the darkness, whispering to myself, "Let them come. I have no place to run to anymore."

Meanwhile, a German came up to Wisia's house and was joined by another. Wisia was standing at the window, so they started asking her whether she had seen a girl or a woman passing by. Wisia replied that she hadn't seen anyone. But they continued asking, because they had seen me making a turn somewhere nearby. But Mrs. Wisia insisted she hadn't seen anyone, even though she had been standing at the window all that time. However, they weren't very insistent and left soon after. After long moments of waiting, full of fear, I looked out, saw that nothing was happening and came out from behind the house.

My behavior must have seemed suspicious to Mrs. Wisia and she might have developed suspicions as to my identity. However, she didn't ask me anything, but just said that the Germans probably wanted to have some fun.

She didn't say anything about this to anyone; at least I didn't feel any ricochets about it from other people. The Tarczyńskis also didn't say anything about these Germans, even though they must have run into them sometime. If so, why had they come here? Were they really looking for someone? But then they would have behaved differently or just stopped by for a moment. Fortunately for me, this dramatic event ended well. At the same time, however, it aroused my dormant fear, my feeling that there was no place where I could feel safe.

Until then, no matter in what place I found myself, the situation always went from bad to worse with the passage of time. Even if nothing serious happened, gradually the atmosphere around me got thicker, preventing me from living peacefully. The same thing began happening in Łąkta. I was still without any documents, and waiting for my *kenkarte* seemed to last forever. Rafał had already started looking for a new place. I don't know if someone said something to him, or perhaps he understood intuitively that I should move out of Łąkta.

While still in the village, I got to know a local girl named Kasia. We took a liking to each other, and from time to time we spent our free hours together. Kasia knew a lot of songs, as did I—from school and Majorek's book of army songs. We sang together or taught each other songs that only one of us knew. It was the end of summer and we would sit under the pear tree in Kasia's garden. We ate pears and sang all kinds of songs. I still remember two of them.

In Łąkta I was hungry almost all the time, also because the mountain air was sharp. I kept eating those pears if only to muffle the hunger. On one occasion I ate a few pears and immediately afterward drank cold water from the well. A female teacher who lived nearby saw me and summed things up, "If this girl doesn't get a horrible stomach ache or typhoid, it will be a miracle." I didn't have even a shadow of stomach ache.

There were forests all around Łąkta, high up above the fields. We went to pick mushrooms, usually the Tarczyńsis and I. I never seemed to have to get the hang of it, perhaps because it was the first time for me. Others followed behind me and picked the mushrooms that I missed.

Occasionally, Mrs. Tarczyńska managed to get milk for her children. To get milk it was necessary to climb high up to one of the farmyards. Even then, however, milk was sometimes inaccessible owing to the prevailing superstitions, such as, when Mrs. Tarczyńska reached the farmyard after sundown, a local woman refused to give her milk, saying if she did, the cows would stop producing it!

I helped Mrs. Tarczyńska in various household chores and took care of the children. The Tarczyński family lived in a former Jewish house, which had been completely stripped of furnishings. They lived very modestly, on the verge of poverty. Despite all this, however, they were cheerful, very decent, and very kind to me.

RETURN TO SŁOMKA

One day, Rafał arrived to take me away from Łąkta. It turned out that my presence there was already the subject of gossip and that Tarczyński had been told that I was Jewish.

It was about 8 p.m. in the fall of 1943 and we traveled to Słomka by foot, via Bochnia. As we arrived, we wondered why the town was so quiet and empty. The streets were empty except for the German patrols, which we avoided. We didn't know that a curfew was in effect and, fortunately, no one stopped us.

I returned to Słomka, to my cubbyhole and, in the meantime, Rafał looked for a new place for me, a place that would be safe and solid. He knew I couldn't remain in Słomka because all that was awaiting me there was this cubbyhole—cold, obscure, and above all, dangerous both for Heniek and myself. He found a new place beyond Tarnów and we went there together. Everything was supposed to be ready.

The Rogalski family, whom Rafał knew from before the war, from his native area, was living in a small locality situated by the railroad. Rafał had run into them by chance, while he was looking for a new abode for me. Mr. Rogalski worked for the railroad, was married, and had two children. He was somewhat of a Semitic type, so that also lent credence to my cover story as a niece from Wielkopolska who had come to stay with them. Rafał told them I was Jewish.

Unfortunately, when we reached the Rogalski's, it transpired that they had changed their minds and refused to take me in. Rafał was very disappointed, but there was nothing he could do about it. We spent the night there and the next day we returned to Bochnia, and from there, to Słomka.

It goes without saying that a mere train ride was very dangerous for me, as well as for Rafał who accompanied me, because I still didn't have my *kenkarte*. Fortunately, this time we managed to avoid the danger from that side, as we didn't run into any German passenger checks or Blue Police.

I continued to live in Słomka, in hiding. It was the first days of November, when the cold had set in, especially at night. Heniek was still working for Wieczorek in slaughter and meat preparation, for which he received food and shelter. They worked whenever they could, without stopping: slaughter, meat preparation, and then the illicit sale. All this activity of course was strictly forbidden by the Germans and could result in the pain of death.

One evening, when the three of us were in the room, several acquaintances of Heniek and Rafał came for a visit. I had to hide immediately lest I encounter them, because they didn't know a young woman was living there. Rafał and Heniek quickly covered me with an eiderdown and blanket and I lay on the edge of the bed close to the wall, while the guests sat on the opposite edge. The whole time the guests were there I had to keep quiet, without moving. I could barely stand it, because I was suffering from a stomach ailment. The situation was very difficult for me and lasted quite a long time. But finally the guests left without noticing that during their visit someone had been lying motionless behind their backs.

Often I felt that I couldn't stand the situation any longer—the constant changes of living quarters, the new, unknown situations. Sometimes I thought that it would be better for me if the end came, unexpectedly, in my sleep, and then I just wouldn't wake up. It seemed to me that I stood no chance of surviving. The period of hiding kept getting longer and each time it was more and more difficult to begin anew. The space seemed to close in around me and the possibilities for rescue kept getting blocked. Who was I running away from anyway? I was running from the Germans, of course, but also from many evil, jealous, and greedy people; also, from who I really was. The pain that couldn't be shown, that just smoldered inside me, burned me with muffled silence, and intensified under the pressure of loneliness. It hurt like pulling out one's fingernails.

Months passed, a year, and then some. "What of it? What was all this for," I thought, "and for whom? Tomorrow, perhaps you won't hold out. Tomorrow, you might slip, someone might denounce you." Depression would take me in its grip and seemed to be saying, "You won't survive. Why all this torment, this struggle, this torture? You don't have anyone. You have lost everything and everyone. What should you live for?"

Many times I was overcome by dejection, lacking the will to go on struggling for my life. There were times, moments, situations when I lived as if I was a robot—Rafał would look for a new place for me and would take me there. Someone else would transport me to a new place. I would get up and go around with my chin pressed against my chest. But I became indifferent to everything, nothing could cheer me up, nothing could encourage me. No experience moved me or prompted me to act. I was too young for all this, and on top of that, I was very sensitive and emotional, which of course did not exactly provide me with a shield against all these experiences. On the contrary—all the experiences left me deeply wounded, and left traces that, even today, don't let me sleep.

Tears—there was no place for them now. On whose shoulder could I cry anyway? Once, a long time ago, there had been Grandmother who I could snuggle up to. I was very timid, even as a young girl, and I refused to sleep alone because I was afraid. I didn't even want to remain in the room in the evening or go someplace outside, so I always had my grandmother or someone else next to me.

And then I sneaked secretly through the fields all by myself, along paths, from the ghetto to Aunt Miecia, and from her, furtively through the fields to Tola, through unknown areas, villages, and roads, filled with the fear of running into someone. I lay alone buried in straw somewhere or under the feeding trough, in a cold cubbyhole, or in some room full of strangers; Night after night I waited in fear, feeling helpless, isolated, and hunted. And I couldn't scream, rebel or cry.

Rafał applied himself assiduously to another search for lodgings or us. It was impossible to go on living clandestinely in Słomka, as everything there was temporary and it was simply impossible for me to go through another winter in this unheated, neglected cubbyhole. During my stay in Łąkta, Rafał had already been looking for a more stable and safe place for me and he had traveled as far as Kraków.

Rafał had also been on the lookout for work for himself to earn our keep, and finally, he managed to land a job in the agricultural school in Opatowiec on Vistula. At first, he went there alone to deal with the formalities and find an apartment for us and by a stroke of luck he came across an acquaintance

Rafał Kałowski with his pupils, c. 1935

of his in the village administration office. It was his former student, Władek Kłoszewski, an organ player whom he had known before the war. Władek was 27 years old and overjoyed to meet his former teacher, promising to help him with everything he could. Władek had arrived in Opatowiec on Vistula as a resettled person and had put down roots—getting engaged to a local girl, playing the organ in the church, and working in the village administration.

Having solved all the formalities, Rafał found an apartment in Opatowiec and returned to Słomka to take me back with him. Heniek stayed behind in Słomka, continuing to work for the Wieczoreks, who agreed to take him in.

IN OPATOWIEC

It was the end of December 1943. It had been 15 months since I went into hiding, fleeing from myself, from my history and identity, from others, and also from my own memory, so that I wouldn't hurt so badly.

Who was I? What was happening to my personality? To what extent was it disappearing, and to what extent had I remained myself? I had had to suppress my personality so many times, as if by force, against myself, and despite myself.

I wasn't myself. I couldn't live with any inner freedom or feel free. Nobody knew who I was, with the exception of Rafał and Heniek. As for the others—Aunt Leszczyńska, Hanna, Maryla, Tola—they couldn't help me with anything because they were far away, not only in the physical sense. No one knew who I was and no one could be allowed to know my true identity. I lived with terrible internal and external loneliness, and all the more so since the tragedy of the loss of my loved ones was inscribed into it. At the same time, paradoxically, life went on as before, day after day, with small hopes and moments of joy.

We arrived in Opatowiec on Christmas Eve, 1943. It was cold, but it wasn't snowing. The distance between Słomka and Opatowiec was 50 kilometers. We had left early in the morning, traveling by rented horse cart, and we reached our destination before dusk.

Despite everything, the village roads and byways were pretty safe. The Germans usually only showed up to check papers when they were carrying out a manhunt or roundups and we traveled without any hitches, with no one stopping us along the way.

Everyone was getting ready for another Christmas under the occupation. It was impossible to predict when the war was going to end, or for how long I would have to remain in hiding. The experiences of 1943 did not bode well, rather they filled me with sorrow and a feeling of hopelessness of what still awaited me. It seemed that hiding would be more and more difficult, while the feeling of impermanence was getting stronger. I was still without official papers, fleeing from one place to another, being forced to forget (in front of others) who I really was. I wondered if I had enough strength and endurance left, if Rafał had enough too, what would befall Heniek who had stayed in Słomka, and for how long I would be able to remain in this new place. All these questions, as well as remembering my loved ones, and recalling past events accompanied me during the journey to Opatowiec.

On arriving in Opatowiec, we first headed for Władek Kłoszewski's, where his fiancée, Fredzia Ćwieluchowa, gave us some bread. Kłoszewski always addressed Rafał with great respect and deference as "Mr. Principal," and with his help Rafał had already rented a room for us. It was a single-story house that was new, large, made of timber, and with rooms in the attic. Our room, or rather kitchen corner, was on the ground floor and next to it were two empty rooms. It was often cold in the room and we would light the stove with bits of old wood because there was no coal. Lilka, the landlady's daughter, and I would go to the nearby woods to gather dry twigs, but because many others also did the same, there was often little to show for our efforts.

The landlady, Mrs. Wawrzykowska, lived next door in a little cottage, together with Lilka, who was slightly older than I was. Their cottage, which was just a kitchen and a little room with a utility building adjoining it, stood deep within the backyard and the house concealed it from view from the road. Our house had been built by another daughter, Dioniza (Dosia) Wiercioch. Dosia lived in Warsaw and was a known publicist with connections in the camp of Polish leader Józef Piłsudski.

Mrs. Wawrzykowska, a widow of many years, was a descendant of an old Opatowiec family. She was a simple woman, but very intelligent and resourceful. She had the gift of a great memory and could recite poems by famous poets. In addition to Dosia and Lilka, Wawrzykowska had two other daughters. One of them, a nurse by occupation, lived with her husband, a baker, in Dębica; the other one, Kazimiera (Kazia) Kling, had gone to Volhynia before the war, but had returned to Opatowiec after fleeing the wave of Ukrainian violence.

Even though Mrs. Wawrzykowska was a widow and had a hard time taking care of herself, she supported her daughters to the best of her ability and had managed to provide her two older daughters with the funds to study in Warsaw. In contrast, the youngest, Lilka, finished only two years of high school before the war began.

Immediately after arriving at the house and unpacking, Kazia Kling, who lived upstairs with her husband, Klemens, and their young son, invited us to a Christmas party. The party itself was very modest and meager. There were only five of us—Klemens and Kazia, their son Kazio, Rafał, and I as his niece.

The Kling family had lived in Wólka, in Volhynia, beyond Rovno. Klemens had worked as a school principal, while Kazimiera, having completed her higher education, was a teacher. He was much older than his wife, introverted, a bit funny, and slightly weird. During the war they had gone through dramatic events. When the Ukrainians in Volhynia started attacking Polish houses and killing Poles, the three of them used to flee to hide among the reeds next to the river, where they would spend the whole night. The Ukrainians usually attacked at night. Without any warning, they would burst into the Polish houses and savagely murder everyone inside. When they came during the day and couldn't find anyone, they looted livestock, furnishings, food, and clothing. They often hid themselves in the farmyard and when the owners came out to feed the cattle or milk the cows, they would burst in and attack them with pitchforks. They often bound the parents and tortured them in front of their children.

After these experiences of constantly hiding among the reeds, and the constant fear of Ukrainian attack, little Kazio developed chronic anxiety. He was four years old at the time and these dramatic experiences inscribed themselves deeply in his mind. Many times, when evening was approaching, he would timidly ask his mother, "Mama, when are we going to the reeds?"

Owing to the efforts of the sister who lived in Dębica, Kazia managed to extricate herself from the inferno of Volhynia. Her brother-in-law, a physician, had some connections among the Germans, paid them a huge amount of money, and succeeded in removing the family from Volhynia. If they had stayed there, they would have been killed for sure, sharing the fate of thousands of other Poles. They arrived in Opatowiec several months ahead of us and kept reliving their dramatic experiences.

They often invited us to their room and despite everything, these evenings were like islands of calm in the sea of the war drama—their resettlement and my hiding. Kazia was endowed with a marvelous sense of humor and kept telling all kinds of jokes and peasant anecdotes, which involved people from all walks of life and professions. They were to the point and very trenchant.

The Klings also became involved with us socially because their relations with her mother, and especially with her sister Lilka, were very tense. Kazia complained constantly about them and it appeared that she wanted us to be on her side in the conflict. This alienated us because we didn't want to participate in family arguments, especially without knowing their origins. In fact, we were being treated very nicely by the Wawrzykowska widow and Lilka was very friendly toward us, so we stopped visiting the Klings. Kazia was aware of everything, especially my friendship with Lilka, and this alienated her from us. Perhaps they also started making guesses about me, because on one occasion little Kazio addressed me as "you little Jew girl."

The conflict between Kazia and Lilka grew more intense and because Lilka was involved with Opatowiec partisans, Kazia threatened her with denouncing Edek Orłowski, Lilka's fiancé. Lilka must have repeated this threat to Edek, because one day some partisans paid a visit to Kazia, demanding her to calm down and stop her threats, or else she would have to face unpleasant consequences. Their warning was sufficient.

In Opatowiec we resumed our efforts to secure a *kenkarte* for me. Władek Kłoszewski had a certificate made for me in the registry and this time my name was Stanisława Kaczmarek, born in Królikowo, in Konin County. Władek gave the new form the stamp of the Opatowiec village administration and then poured coffee on the new document. Seeing him doing this, Rafał moaned, "Władek, Władek, what have you done? What will this document look like now?"

"It's alright," replied Władek. "Don't you worry, Mr. Principal, everything will be alright."

The document did, in fact, acquire a "worn out" look. As it came to light later, Władek had many similar incidences "on his conscience," and knew how to properly forge and prepare documents. In Opatowiec he knew people, played the organ, and worked as a bookkeeper, which made him a prestigious figure in the little town, and provided him with a sense of security in his underground work. He also helped with procuring forged documents for people in hiding.

Sabina Kałowska, ID photo, c. 1946

We went to the village administration office with him. "Why don't you finish this *kenkarte* business already?" Władek asked his female work colleague.

"Why, is this an acquaintance of yours?" she replied.

"Of course," he said. "I've known her since she was little."

The real Stanisława Kaczmarek, a resettled person from the Poznań region, did indeed live somewhere near Łąkta and Władek had known her from childhood. And so, after waiting three months, I finally received my *kenkarte*. With this *kenkarte*, issued in the name of Stanisława Kaczmarek, I survived until the end of the war.

In Opatowiec, Rafał worked in an agricultural school, while I usually remained at home. Mrs. Wawrzykowska had a goat, which was always tied near the little barn or near her cottage and behind the cottage she had a plot of land where she grew tobacco. She had another little plot outside of town, near the forest, where she grew potatoes. In the spring I helped with the tobacco, during the summer harvest Lilka and I worked in the field belonging to her fiancé's family, the affluent Orłowskis, tying bundles of hay, and in the fall I helped dig potatoes.

Tobacco was a very precious commodity during the war, which is why many people grew it clandestinely, even on tiny plots. It was transported by hiding the leaves under one's clothes. People traded in practically everything. Everyone who could was into trading something. Rafał also tried his hand at trading—he traveled to Kraków, or took a boat up the Vistula River to Koszyce, where he would buy a packet of saccharine and then sell it in smaller packets, thereby yielding a little profit. Or, when as a teacher he got his allocation of vodka or cigarettes, he would sell them for a small profit and buy saccharine. He wasn't good at this and usually, instead of a profit there was a great deal of laughter. He would buy saccharine and then sell it for the same price, thinking that it wasn't proper to make a profit on this or that acquaintance of his. He spent money on merchandise and travel expenses and then had nothing to repeat the entire operation. In effect, he almost always drew a bad bargain. But in general, this trade generated a little money. However, daily life was very difficult and once Rafał had to sell his pants just to make ends meet. On another occasion, he sold a gold watch chain that his brother had given him.

Opatowiec was a very picturesque town located on the left, higher bank of the Vistula River vis-à-vis the confluence of the Vistula and Dunajec, where the waters of the two rivers—the willow-green of the Dunajec and the gray of the Vistula—mixed together. At some places, the bank of the river on the Opatowiec side was very steep with deep ancient basements. There was a harbor where commercial and coal barges docked, as well as a little passenger boat, which shuttled people between Opatowiec and Kraków. On the opposite side of the river was a village called Ujście Jezuickie, from where one could cross to Opatowiec by a little ferryboat.

Partisan units of various affiliations were very active in the Opatowiec area. There was a large unit of Peasant Battalions (Bataliony Chłopskie), called "*Wicher*" (storm), as well as units of the Home Army (AK) and the National Armed Forces (NSZ).

We befriended two brothers, Władysław and Jan Pociej, who lived in town. Before the war, Władysław had apparently been the youngest lawyer in Poland, who had gotten his license and started practicing when he was just 24 years old. Rafał was close with the older brother, Jan, who was 28 then. He had completed his studies in agronomy before the war. During the occupation he settled in Opatowiec and from the end of 1939 and through 1940 he was a church organ player. Jan Pociej came to visit us quite often and conducted long conversations with Rafał on the military and politics. Their cousin, Stefania Kawka, who was also called Stefa or Stenia, also lived in Opatowiec. She lived with a man who survived in hiding under the name of Władysław Kret and taught at clandestine study groups. Jan Pociej arranged forged documents for him and only after the war I learned that his true name was Wilhelm Szewczyk, a well-known writer and publicist from Silesia. Stefania once composed a poem about Opatowiec, which we sang to a very well-known German melody.

Newspapers and bulletins from underground organizations were distributed among acquaintances and trusted persons. They also reached Rafał who, in turn, passed them on to me. Now and then he brought me a book to read. Of all those that I read, I was moved most deeply by Sienkiewicz's *Quo Vadis*.

The atmosphere that prevailed in Opatowiec was completely different from that of other places in which I had stayed. One could feel here some kind of human solidarity, a common bond in the struggle and resistance against the Germans, the presence of partisans, and even simple kindness. Everything was a pretext for building social and friendship bonds. There were no betrayals or denunciations here. For example, there was a poor milkman living in town who took care of a little girl. People talked about her being Jewish and even told me about her, but no one denounced her throughout the war.

Partisans were based in the nearby forests, but they had their own people in Opatowiec, which served as their home front, providing night lodgings and living quarters, while supplying information about German movements and planned operations. Members of underground organizations lived in various houses, weapons were stored, and drop boxes were operative. Effective and skillful air drops of weapons and equipment from England took place in the area. At night we often heard the rumble of airplanes arriving to drop supplies and would wake up to see what was happening. Later, the secret caches of weapons were carried on horse carts to barns and other hiding places. One such barn containing air-dropped equipment was located almost opposite our house, on the other side of the road.

People warned each other about approaching German danger. For example, Mr. Czarnecki, who worked in the post office, would sometimes intercept German communications via telephone and he immediately passed on the overheard information to the partisans and the town residents. We were usually warned by Janek Pociej and Roma Czarnecka, who later married Ćwieluch, the brother of Władek Kłoszewski. Whenever danger was imminent, Władek himself would rush to our house, knock on the window, and yell, "Mr. Principal, run, the Germans are coming!" and be on his way again, adjusting his spectacles; he was also on the run because of his extensive involvement in forging birth certificates, *kenkarten*, and other documents. Once, when he was in a hurry, he dropped his glasses, returned to pick them up, and ran again. In such cases, we would all run to the forest. When things calmed down, someone from the town would notify us and we would return.

IMPRISONMENT AND RESCUE OF HENIEK

In March 1944, news reached us about Heniek's and Mr. Wieczorek's arrest in Słomka and their imprisonment in Kraków.

A pretty girl named Edzia, who worked in the village administration office in Krzeszów, knew that Heniek concealed his true name and assumed a false one. However, she believed that Heniek was in hiding for political reasons. At that time, Heniek was hiding—and did so until the end of the war—under the assumed name of Tola's brother, Julek Grzywnowicz, who was in Germany doing forced labor. The Germans had actually grabbed and arrested his sister Tola, but he had volunteered to go instead of her. On the basis of his documents, Heniek got his residence registry in Słomka and then a *kenkarte*. Miss Edzia took a liking to Heniek and they began to meet. But a former student from Vilno, who had also once helped Wieczorek in his clandestine work, started making things difficult for Heniek and Heniek acted negligently by provoking this young man's jealousy, which, under the prevailing conditions, involved a considerable risk. This former student was Heniek's age, also tall and handsome, and he had courted Edzia prior to Heniek. (He had also once tried to date me, but without success.) At some point he became jealous of Heniek and, after searching for an opportunity to take revenge, he talked his two brothers into attacking Heniek. The attack took place while on his way back from meeting with Edzia and he reached Wieczorek's house with a bleeding head.

Then, in February, some Germans pulled up at Wieczorek's house and arrested both Heniek and Wieczorek. Boguś, a Gestapo man from Bochnia and originally from Silesia, also showed up. Boguś was an informant and a villain who was later shot to death by partisans. He started screaming, "What, you are slaughtering animals illegally, while German soldiers on the front have nothing to eat?!"

During the arrest, Mrs. Wieczorek showed uncommon courage and replied sharply, "We didn't want this war!"

"But there is a war on," he roared, "and here you are doing illegal butchery! You, monkey, on the floor," he shouted, as he pointed his pistol at her.

Heniek and Wieczorek were taken away, transported to Kraków and imprisoned in the St. Michael prison. Heniek's situation became nearly hopeless. All prisoners had to go through the so-called quarantine, where his origins would be revealed. Until then Wieczorek hadn't known the truth about Heniek and Heniek decided to come clean about himself. When they were alone in the cell, he said, "Mr. Wieczorek, I am a Jew."

"Jesus Christ and Holy Mary, I have a wife and children! What's going to happen now?" Wieczorek exclaimed.

In quarantine the guard would call out the prisoner's name and he would step forward. When he read the name Grzywnowicz, Heniek did not step forward, pretending he hadn't heard. There was some commotion and he managed to slip away and ultimately avoid going through quarantine, which literally saved him.

But the adversities seemed without end. While waiting for his trial on charges of illegal slaughter, an anonymous denunciation arrived at the prison, saying that Heniek was in hiding for political reasons. One can only guess that this denunciation had been made by a jealous student. The Germans started interrogating Heniek, conducted a political investigation, and checked his papers. However, the investigators failed to uncover the fact that his *kenkarte* was issued under the false name of Julian Grzywnowicz and concluded that the *kenkarte* was genuine and that Heniek was who he claimed to be. He was interrogated, beaten, and subjected to blackmail in order to make him reveal names and contacts, on the promise that he would be released, but he didn't say a word.

Meanwhile, in Bochnia, a rumor started making the rounds—the reason was unclear—that Heniek was Jewish. A family of intelligentsia (both were teachers), who had an illegal radio set, lived in Bochnia and Rafał and Heniek used to go to them to listen to the Allied broadcasts and copy news items onto flyers, which were then passed on to others. When they heard about Heniek they said that after the war they would hang Kałowski for having brought a Jew to them, because now, when he was under arrest, he would "spill" everything, including listening to underground radio broadcasts. They were convinced that Heniek would betray them. However, afterwards they remembered him with great respect, saying he was a noble person who hadn't betrayed anyone.

The news of Wieczorek's and Heniek's arrests reached us in Opatowiec very quickly. We knew what this could result in if the course of things took a turn for the worse. Both of them were to be put on trial for clandestine, illegal slaughter and trade. Simultaneously, an investigation was going on against Heniek in the context of his political activities as described in the anonymous denunciation.

Rafał went to Kraków and found a lawyer for Heniek. Mrs. Wieczorek arrived for the trial, but Rafał wasn't able to attend. During the trial, Heniek was very pale and looked dreadful after the numerous rounds of interrogation and torture related to his alleged political activity. Wieczorek was convicted of illegal slaughter and trade, but Heniek wasn't sentenced because the second, political investigation was still going on. Heniek told Mrs. Wieczorek that he had no chance of release because he was being held for political crimes, and that he awaited execution. Throughout this time, no one in the prison system or the police knew that Heniek was Jewish.

One day the guard called out the name Grzywnowicz. Heniek got up and said goodbye to his fellow prisoners, convinced he was going to his death. But he was led through the hallways of the prison in the direction of the gate. The gate was opened and he was let out! They had failed to gather evidence of Heniek's alleged political activity and closed the case.

The night before his unexpected release, Heniek had had a dream in which the sun was shining constantly… And all of a sudden he found himself outside the prison, a free man, without quite believing what had happened. He walked around Kraków for half a day as if intoxicated, half conscious, and felt as if he had experienced his own death. He was released without warning after five months. Wieczorek had also been released not long before.

During Heniek's imprisonment, Rafał ran around in circles trying to get help. He went to see Heniek's lawyer in Kraków many times. It goes without saying that I couldn't visit him there. Instead, I prepared parcels for Heniek, which Roma Czarnecka took to Kraków. I didn't have any money to buy food, so I paid Roma with my dress and shoes in exchange for food and cigarettes. During Roma's visits Heniek asked about us, how things were going, and above all, for cigarettes.

After this unexpected, indeed, miraculous release from prison, Heniek tried to reach us in Opatowiec as quickly as possible. First, he went to see the Grzegorek couple, who still lived in Jodłówka, near Bochnia. He had with him a gold ring, which had belonged to his mother, my grandmother. Grandmother had taken it off and given it to him at the last moment, at the fairgrounds in Jędrzejów, where the Germans had gathered the Jews from the ghetto before transporting them to the camp in Treblinka. After his stint in prison Heniek was completely "naked"—he had nothing, not a penny to travel to Opatowiec. The Grzegorek couple refused to lend him money for travel, so he gave them the ring, the only souvenir of his mother and his entire childhood and adolescence in the house of his parents. Needless to say, the Grzegorek couple gave him just enough money to get to us. He nursed resentment against them because of their unwillingness to help and their mistrust. After the war he tried to locate them to recover the ring, the most precious souvenir of his mother, but to no avail.

One day, after harvest, at the end of July, Władek Kłoszewski burst into our apartment, yelling, "Mr. Principal, Miss Dzidka, come quickly! Mr. Julek is on the other side of the river and is waiting for a boat to cross over to our side!"

It was Heniek, of course, who went by the name of Julek Grzywnowicz. I hurried to the riverbank and could see him standing on the opposite bank, even though the river was very wide there. After many months of being apart and the tremendous anxiety about his survival, to this day I cherish the image of his small figure above the gray surface of the water. I started waving and crying. There was a little harbor with a ferryman and he transported us across the river. On seeing Heniek again, I was overwhelmed with emotion and after the long months of separation, which indeed seemed to be heading for a tragic end, I wouldn't let him out of my embrace. Our joy was indescribable. After all, he was the person closest to me, the only one of our family to survive the annihilation. He didn't look good. The pants that he'd taken from Rafał were almost threadbare and his shoes were worn out, held together with wire, and everything he wore was full of lice after the prison. After we got home, I put all his clothes into a large laundry pot to wash and boil. But we were together once again and Heniek began to live with us in Opatowiec.

TOGETHER IN OPATOWIEC

On April 1, 1944, I succeeded in playing a trick on Mrs. Wawrzykowska. She had a goat that was always tied to a stake in the backyard and one day I burst into the kitchen of the small house, shouting, "Mrs. Wawrzykowska, do you know what happened? The goat escaped from the backyard."

"What?! What did you say?"

She dashed outside to see for herself what had happened to the goat and returned a moment later, yelling, "Just you wait, you goat, I'll give it to you!"

"April Fool," I replied, laughing.

Mrs. Wawrzykowska was very open and lively, and had a great sense of humor. After the war we saw each other once, when she came to visit me in Wrocław.

Opatowiec, summer, 1943. Lidia Irena Krajewska (third from left), murdered by the Germans in June, 1944; Lidia (Lilka) Wawrzykowska (right).

Jan Pociej visited us quite often, bringing with him underground flyers, which I read. Of course no one in Opatowiec knew what Rafał was really doing and they kept suggesting that he join the active underground.

Jan Pociej invited me for a stroll several times. I excused myself as best I could, explaining that I had nothing to wear. However, on one occasion I agreed to meet with him. I put on Rafał's fur coat and went to the appointed spot. We strolled on top of the dike, towards the forest, and went together to the church. Throughout all this, Jan was very kind to me.

One day, I don't remember if it was April or May, the Germans grabbed Lilka and transported her to Nowy Korczyn, ten kilometers down the river, for forced labor. Later, Nowy Korczyn acquired notoriety; in 1944 the front stopped there for six months. The Russians spent a long time there. Lilka spent just a few days in Korczyn, escaped, and returned to Opatowiec. Afterwards, she had to be very alert and cautious to avoid falling into the hands of the Germans, and when the situation got dangerous she would flee or hide with us.

The house in which we lived didn't have a basement, but it was slightly elevated and there was a big enough space between the ground and the floor to hide. A pantry adjoined our room and through it one could reach this hiding place beneath the house. From the outside, on the backyard side, our room was adjoined by a little hallway from which one could enter straight into our room. Other doors led to the adjoining room, which also had another door to the hallway and from there to the veranda, which faced the nearby cemetery. Rafał built an "emergency" passage to the space under the floor and one could easily lift two planks and enter the space beneath the floor to hide.

Lilka knew, of course, about this hideout and once she burst into our room in a panic, because a German expedition had started conducting a search in town. Lilka was very afraid after her escape from forced labor and went to hide under our floor.

I was also scared, but couldn't hide together with Lilka because I had no reason to. I was Stanisława Kaczmarek with a *kenkarte* and had no reason to be afraid. It goes without saying that Lilka didn't know who I really was and therefore any unjustified behavior on my part was liable to arouse her suspicions and that of others. So Lilka hid under our floor, I put the planks back in their place, and we waited for the danger to pass.

In May 1944, another problem arose, this time a health problem: My front tooth started going bad. The very strange Danielewicz family lived in Opatowiec. They were Armenian and the Germans had resettled them from the east. It wasn't clear how they landed in Opatowiec, but it was known that they were in cahoots with the Germans. In 1945, they also fled together with the Germans due to the advancing Soviet troops. As he was a dentist I went to him with my bad tooth, but he didn't want to fix it, just extract it. I was in despair. "I am still young and if I lose a front tooth, I will look terrible all my life," I wailed. I fought for the tooth, as if I were convinced I'd survive and live a long time.

Rafał found out that a dental technician lived somewhere in Koszyce and I decided to take the chance. I set out for Koszyce by foot, 16 kilometers each way. I had only one pair of light shoes and to avoid ruining them completely, I took them off and walked to Koszyce barefoot. The dental technician said he would give it a try and that the tooth wasn't a total loss. The treatment lasted a long time—he cleaned the root, drained the pus, and put some kind of lotion on it.

I walked barefoot to Koszyce and back many times and I often met Germans on the way, but they never stopped me to check my identity. In any event, I already had my *kenkarte*, which gave me a feeling of safety; never completely, but still I felt much safer than during the time I had had no official papers whatsoever. They often started talking to me and even offered me a ride in a car or a horse cart, but invariably I thanked them politely and continued on my way. I preferred to walk barefoot than to ride with them. Finally, after a long course of treatment, my tooth was cured and it remains in its place to this day.

In the spring and summer of 1944 the partisans grew bolder, often entering the town quite openly. One day several partisans in full uniform entered the town from the forest side, passing by the cemetery, and heading for the Armenian dentist. By pure chance several Nazis were also passing by. There was one German and three Ukrainians on the horse cart; all of them were armed and carried ammunition. Both sides almost ran into each other while leaving the protection of the cemetery wall. The partisans responded first by throwing grenades at the soldiers, jumping over the wall and withdrawing into the woods. The entire operation unfolded in our neighborhood; Lilka and I heard the explosions and shooting and we ran outside to see what was going on. The outcome was that the partisans withdrew and the soldiers continued on their way in the direction of the Opatowiec market square. However, one scared Ukrainian fled into Mrs. Wawrzykowska's tobacco plot. Later, we saw him dragging himself out of there, without a hat, and glasses askew. He was like a scared rabbit.

After half an hour, perhaps longer, a whole unit of heavily armed partisans arrived in Opatowiec. The Nazis barricaded themselves in the post office, which was located in the side alley leading from the market square. They telephoned their people and told them about the developing situation and requested help. The Nazis had automatic weapons and a whole box of ammunition, which they had brought with them on the cart, and they took the post office workers as hostages. The partisans, for their part, surrounded the town and the area of the market square.

The town's residents started to flee, as it seemed like a large battle was shaping up. Those who had hidden weapons began pulling them out in order to reinforce the partisan battalion. I went to the Czarnecki's, who lived near the market square, to get some bread. Thus, instead of fleeing I found myself right in the middle of the action. On meeting an acquaintance, he asked, "What are you doing here? Why aren't you escaping?"

"Because I have to go to Czarnecki's to get bread," I replied.

"Don't you know that partisans are everywhere and things are getting hot? Run!" he said.

And yet I stayed. Shooting was going on all around me and I found myself in the middle of the battle, somewhere near the post office. I hid behind a wall and watched the battle.

The partisans found it difficult to seize the post office, because the Nazis had barricaded themselves in well and were shooting from all directions with automatic weapons through small windows with bars. A young partisan, deputy commander of the unit, dropped dead in front of me after he emerged from the protection of the wall in order to lob a grenade. His name was Linczewski, his *nom de guerre* was Rybka. He was a native of Silesia. "Good Lord, what have you done?!" I yelled to the partisan who was standing right next to me.

"We have started the harvest," he replied.

"Isn't it too early?" I asked.

"It's about time," was his answer.

The Nazis defended themselves stubbornly. Finally, however, the partisans overran the post office building, getting inside through the roof and then the attic. One frightened Ukrainian hid in the basement. Another one managed to flee to a potato field. But a German whom they found still in the post office retained his pride and arrogance, "I was alone and you were many, and still you couldn't make it," he mocked. "I fought at Stalingrad and have a decoration," he boasted. Later, the partisans shot him to death outside of town and took his boots.

Suddenly, Lilka was standing right next to me. "Well, this time our people gave them a good beating," she said.

One partisan who was wounded in action turned out to be the commander and was carried to our house. He was put in bed in the unoccupied room that adjoined ours. Young women who served with the partisans as medics came to our house, but they had no medical supplies with them and just kept running around, causing a commotion. So I started making bandages from bed sheets and shirts. The commander's hand had been wounded. A doctor came from Nowy Korczyn and took care of him. The fallen soldier was also brought to us. He was laid on a door that was removed from its frame that linked our room with the next one. The dead partisan was with us the entire night.

Shortly afterwards German reinforcements arrived, but the town was well prepared for defense and the Germans had to withdraw without overcoming the partisans. That night the partisans remained in town to defend the residents from the likely arrival of larger German forces. They withdrew into the woods the next morning, taking their wounded commander with them. The next day, some young men took the fallen partisan to the cemetery and temporarily interred him in a burial chamber. Lilka and I put flowers on his grave. We also washed the door and the entire room in order not to leave any traces. Everyone was convinced that the Germans would certainly return with larger forces and settle scores with the civilian population. For this reason everyone fled to the woods and the cliffs over the Vistula River. The Germans did, in fact, enter the town and fanned out in every direction. They went to the cemetery and found the body of the fallen partisan and saw the fresh flowers on the grave, but they left the body alone. They also came to our house but they found no one there, and neither did they find traces of any partisans.

Fortunately, they did not take revenge against the population of Opatowiec, as was their habit. They must have reached the conclusion that the perpetrators were "bandits from the woods" and the local population had not taken part in the events. That day Opatowiec looked like a ghost town. Finally, the Germans left and only then could we return to our houses. The following day, the residents of Opatowiec arranged a proper funeral for the fallen partisan and interred him in a grave.

The weather in the summer of 1944 was beautiful, warm, and sunny. Partisans kept launching bold attacks in the area, surprising the Germans in various localities and attacking army posts and convoys. We heard the sounds of shooting all the time and learned about new operations.

Little steamboats shuttled regularly between Opatowiec and Kraków. One day I set out with Rafał to Koszyce, taking the boat upriver. It was my first time and, as it turned out, also the last. In the afternoon, as we were returning to Opatowiec we passed another riverboat, which was heading upriver in the direction of Kraków. The captain of the other boat, which had departed some time before from Opatowiec, warned our captain not to proceed further because something was happening in town, that shooting had been heard. "Probably partisans fighting it out with the Germans," he said.

Our captain disregarded the warning, saying, "It doesn't matter. The partisans will have taken care of them before we arrive. If the Germans try to do something, the partisans will intervene and won't let them."

He was very sure of himself and we kept on going. When we reached Opatowiec, the captain began maneuvering the steamboat in the direction of the dock. Suddenly, the Germans began lobbing grenades towards the boat. Acting quickly, the captain backed up and stopped the boat in the middle of the river.

We spent the whole night on the steamboat, which was anchored in the middle of the Vistula. The boat was terribly infected with vermin and the bugs bit every single passenger. Some of them panicked, thinking that the Germans would sink the boat. The fighting in Opatowiec lasted all night. We heard shooting and saw the flames from the burning houses. Opatowiec turned into a scene of slaughter. The town was burning and the Germans were hard at work, murdering the residents. Some residents managed to reach the riverbank. They hid in the caves, which had been dug out of the escarpment; the priest Paweł Widerski was also with them. The Germans captured the church and built a machine gun nest on its tower, from which they shot everyone they saw. However, during their retreat they didn't set fire to the church.

It turned out that a Ukrainian unit, which was retreating together with the Germans from the Lublin area in the east, was passing through Opatowiec. There were about 400 soldiers all told, Ukrainians and Germans, and they stopped there and made camp. Having learned of the situation, the partisans moved toward Opatowiec, surrounded the camp, and launched an attack. They killed three Ukrainians, but very quickly realized that their numbers and firepower were not enough to overcome the Ukrainians' resistance. The attack broke down and the partisans, no longer able to defend themselves and unable to count on reinforcements because the remaining units were engaged in operations elsewhere, began to retreat. And so they left the town to the mercies of the Germans and Ukrainians who, driven by a desire for revenge, began settling scores with Opatowiec's residents in the most savage fashion. They started fires and murdered people; they shot at everything that moved—people and animals. Anyone who came outside or tried to sneak through the streets was shot. Those who fled to their basement were asphyxiated by fire and smoke, because the henchmen set fire to houses and lobbed grenades into the basements. They left Opatowiec only at noon the next day, when they were done with the massacre.

It was then, after a sleepless night in the middle of the river, and having witnessed the tragedy of the town, that we finally docked. Opatowiec looked ghastly—smoldering ruins, hot flames, human bodies, and the carcasses of horses and cows. The stench of burning and billowing smoke was everywhere. With despair in our eyes and hearts, we crossed the market square and the little streets, in the direction of our house.

Opatowiec began to count its losses and bandage its wounded. Thirty people, aged 3 to 83, perished, and several dozen were wounded. The survivors despaired over the loss of their loved ones, the loss of their homes, and the destruction of their property.

Among the victims of the savagery were people we knew. Terenia, a beautiful 16-year-old girl, was killed. The Germans had wanted to rape her, she resisted, and they murdered her. Lidia Irena Krajewska, aged 18, was also murdered, as was Alfreda Pućińska, aged 17. Many young women were raped, but not killed. Some victims were dragged out of their houses or basements. Two Baczyński family members were killed—Bronisław, the father, and his only son, Ignacy.

Luckily for us, our house was left intact. After the operation was over, a Ukrainian who was setting fire to the house was called to another site at the last minute. Mrs. Wawrzykowska started putting out the fire. Władek Kłoszewski wasn't around at that time; right from the start he had fled somewhere and hidden from the Germans.

As quickly as possible a common burial ceremony for the victims was arranged; hastily assembled wooden coffins were placed next to each other with the victims inside. Everyone—families, acquaintances, and relatives—painfully felt the tragedy they had witnessed. The mood at the cemetery was deeply moving. A detachment of partisans dressed in black coats and bearing arms came from the woods to the funeral. "*Rota*" was sung. German planes made threatening rounds in the sky, but nobody moved.

Rafał and I survived, thanks to our voyage to Koszyce. On that tragic day, no one could have known for certain whether he would live to see another day. The town licked its wounds, unable to forget the tragedy it had endured.

After the tragedy, several new families, whose homes had been destroyed, settled in our house. Among them were the Orłowski family—the father, mother, and Edek, Lilka's fiancé—who until then were one of the more affluent families in town. Their house had burned down completely and so they took up residence in the room adjoining ours.

In August 1944, not long after the notorious massacre, a detachment of German engineering corps was stationed in Opatowiec. They wore yellow uniforms and built trenches, barbed-wire entanglements, and prepared the town to be on the defensive front line. Every day they took people for manual labor—piling up ramparts, digging trenches, stretching barbed wire, and preparing defense lines.

The Germans went from house to house, selecting men. Heniek and Rafał were recruited for work, as was Lilka's fiancé, Edek Orłowski. People tried to wriggle out of it by not reporting for work or going into hiding. One day the Germans grabbed Lilka and me and forced us to dig trenches. Because there were no shovels, someone went off to bring them, and we were supposed to wait. Taking advantage of the general commotion, we fled to a nearby cornfield and then walked across the fields back home. From then on, we were more cautious and started hiding so as to avoid falling into German hands.

Lilka was involved in the illegal distillation of alcohol, or *bimber* as it was commonly known. This was a very profitable enterprise, which she didn't do at her place, but rather in the little hallway adjoining our room. All the machinery was set up there, plus the leaven from the potatoes from which she made the alcohol, as well as the containers with pure *bimber*.

At that time, the soldiers of the engineering corps were recruiting men for manual labor. Their leader was a German nicknamed "Red Ganz," on account of his blond-red hair. He terrified everyone, beat up whoever fell into his hands, terrorized the workers digging trenches, and tormented them savagely. Everyone who came into contact with him told hair-raising stories. I didn't know him personally, but the frightening stories were enough to fear him.

One day, when Lilka was at work distilling *bimber*, some Germans started banging at the front door. Lilka immediately went down to the hideout underneath the floor, Heniek and Edek fled instantly, and Rafał wasn't at home at the time, as he had left earlier for Koszyce or Kraków. Everyone absconded and I went ahead to open the door. I don't know why I didn't escape with the others. There were three of them standing at the door: Red Ganz, whom I recognized instantly, and two others. They entered and, of course, immediately noticed the distillation machinery. "*Aha, ganze bimber fabrik. Wo ist direktor*?" ("Aha, a complete *bimber* factory. Where is the manager?") It was obvious to them that I couldn't produce alcohol all by myself.

"He is not here," I replied.

"Maria Wawrzykowska?" they asked, thinking this was me.

They had been searching for Lilka ever since she had escaped from doing manual labor.

"No!" I answered.

They kept looking around. They saw a plaque on our door with the name Kałowski inscribed on it.

"Where is he?" one asked.

"He is not here," I said.

They looked into the room, which was, of course, empty. There was quiet in the house, nothing could be heard.

"And who is with you?" they kept asking.

"I don't know," I replied.

I replied calmly and confidently as if I wasn't aware of the present and clear danger. One of them was a Ukrainian who spoke a little Polish and he asked the questions, translating for Red Ganz.

"And who else is involved?" he asked once again.

"I don't know," I said again.

"So you are doing it by yourself?" he asked.

They presumed that I was involved. After all, they had caught me in the act—pure *bimber* was trickling slowly into a glass container. But they kept asking about another person, because they guessed—correctly—that I couldn't cope alone with the complicated work involved in alcohol distillation. They kept looking around but, of course, they didn't find anyone. Fortunately, they weren't very inquisitive or aggressive. After all, they could have easily shown their brutality and started hitting me.

At that moment, without quite knowing why, I asked him, "Are you the person from the work detail?"

"I am from the Gestapo. And how come you never come to work?" he asked.

"Someone else from the family goes," I replied.

"And what is your name?" he enquired.

"Dzidka," I replied.

"Dzidka, give us some glasses. We'll have a drink," he demanded.

"I don't have any glasses," I said. "But I'll get some for you."

I dashed off to Mrs. Wawrzykowska. I thought that if they had asked for glasses, then the situation could not be very bad. Mrs. Wawrzykowska knew about the arrival of the German patrol and was all atremble.

"Mrs. Wawrzykowska," I said as I burst into her house, "give me some drinking glasses and some *hors d'oeuvres* and bring them to the large house. Perhaps they will just have a drink, eat a bite, and leave."

I returned and Mrs. Wawrzykowska followed me a moment later. But when they saw her, they didn't want to have a drink on the premises. They just yelled at me, "Bring us bottles!"

"I don't have any bottles," I replied.

To this day, I have no idea how I summoned such boldness. I was almost brazen. It's strange that none of them hit me. In any event, one of them noticed a liter bottle standing in the corner. I didn't want to give it to them—as if I really could want or not want something. But they took it themselves, filled it with *bimber* and left. And I just stood there in disbelief.

It was astonishing that this incident had a happy ending, as far as I was concerned. Lilka, who had been underneath the floor all that time, as well as Heniek and Edek who had been under the window outside, expected the worst. They had been waiting for the Nazis to start beating me. They said they had been ready to go inside if the Germans had started hitting me or had even behaved aggressively.

In such unexpected situations, I behaved as if I had forgotten I was in serious danger. Even though I was paralyzed with fear, I kept my cool and self-confidence, which might have served as a kind of shield. Thanks to that, I managed to wriggle out of many dangerous situations. It was as if I drew attention away from myself, dispelling suspicions which might have arisen had I started showing fear and getting all twisted up in my answers or testimonies.

After this near disaster, Lilka did not shut down her business, but rather moved the machinery to the attic of her small cottage where she lived with her mother. Two days later the Nazis came back. "How is our Dzidka the *bimber* maker? Are you still by yourself?" they asked. They searched for the machinery in vain. They didn't find anything.

In Opatowiec in the spring of 1944, work continued on establishing the front line. The Germans planned to surround the entire town with trenches and barbed-wire entanglements. The school Rafał had worked at was closed by the

Germans at the beginning of the school year, in the fall of 1944, so every day he and Heniek went to work on construction of the German defense lines. We sensed that the end of the war was approaching, even though we still had to wait a long time for that to happen. The Germans did not carry out any more roundups and only the technical and engineering corps were still stationed in town. I, too, started doing manual labor. The workers were issued a ration of bread with marmalade. The Germans guarded their trenches, fortifications, and wire entanglements against reprisal. During the offensive of winter 1945, their fortifications turned into a trap as they retreated quickly under the surge of the Soviet offensive and they fell into their own entanglements and trenches.

One day, in the fall of 1944, Lilka and I went to the woods. At the edge of the forest, we dug up some potatoes from Wawrzykowska's plot and decided to make a fire to bake them in the ashes. Searching for firewood, we went a little deeper into the woods. All at once some partisans appeared, but in order not to be recognized and to scare us they spoke German to us. They chased us away, saying that wandering around this area was forbidden. That was the first time I ever saw partisans in the forest. A little scared, we returned to the field where some acquaintances with whom we had dug up the potatoes were waiting for us.

In Opatowiec, I didn't feel as lonely as in other places I had stayed; Rafał was almost always nearby and then Heniek, who had returned from prison in Kraków, remained with me to the end. In addition to them, I also had many acquaintances. They were candid, and not as introverted, mistrustful or jealous as the people I had met previously. The atmosphere in town, even a small one like Opatowiec, and where many people had connections with the underground, was different from that in remote villages. Also, the social climate in the Kraków area was different from that in the Kielce countryside.

Lilka, who had become my best friend, was very much attached to her fiancé, Edek Orłowski. Edek was very handsome and about the same age as Lilka. One night, when the town became the scene of another operation and there was shooting on the streets, she dashed off to see him, to warn him, and to see for herself that nothing had happened to him.

During a certain period Edek started looking at me and tried to flirt with me once or twice. I stopped him very quickly, saying, "Mr. Edek, you know what? Lilka is my friend and you shouldn't try this with me." Edek and Lilka got married after the war and later left for Western Poland, to Nowa Sola. I never saw them again.

To preempt other flirt attempts, I publicized the fact that I was already engaged, and when Heniek returned from prison I told everybody that my fiancé was back. The presence of Rafał, whom everybody considered my uncle, explained the fact why my "fiancé" lived with us. Together we formed a complementary triangle—Rafał as my uncle, Heniek as my fiancé, and I. In fact, it was the opposite—Rafał was my fiancé and Heniek was my uncle.

After the tragic fire in Opatowiec, several families moved in to our "large" house, which got very crowded and constricted. In addition to the Orłowskis, the Wiewiór family also took up residence there. He had worked as a prosecutor before the war, in Kraków or Silesia, and he liked to drink. When he was "toasted" he liked to play pranks; for example, he would kneel in front of Mrs. Wawrzykowska. His wife bore her husband's drunken performances in silence and only later, when he sobered up, did she remind him of all that he had done while drunk. But he would not believe her and would deny everything; he simply couldn't remember anything.

Another family that moved into our house was Władek Kłoszewski and his wife. Her family's house, where they had been living until then, was burned to the ground by the Germans. After the war, they returned to Władek's native region of Poznań.

The food situation was getting worse; there were practically no stores and there was nothing to buy anyway. Food was acquired in many different ways—through purchases made in the villages by bartering or trading. Whoever had a cow sold the milk and butter and lived on the proceeds. Everything was in demand, especially potatoes, tobacco, saccharine, and vodka. More resourceful residents grew rich from the food trade. Sly peasants from the villages surrounding Opatowiec did good business transporting food to Kraków, where it was possible to sell food with great ease and for almost any price. Krakówians paid for food with gold, jewelry, other valuables, and furniture. One could get a piano for a piece of pork fat! Stefania, a cousin of the Pociejs, composed a poem on this subject and we used to recite it with great laughter. In truth, many peasants made profits from the war.

Christmas of 1944 was very modest. During the preceding days I helped Władek Kłoszewski bake holiday wafers. We prepared some dough, which was then baked in a hot metal baking dish. Even though everyone knew that the front would start moving soon and the end of the war was soon possible, there wasn't any mood of joy or enthusiasm. Everyone was tired of the years of war and occupation. Everyone had experienced terrible things, the deaths of loved ones or friends, everyone was tired from the harsh reality of everyday life. On Christmas Eve there were five of us: Heniek, Rafał and I, Mrs. Wawrzykowska, and Lilka. A modest meal awaited us on the table. We had managed to get some flour and I managed to make some macaroni.

The entire house was enveloped by a mood of sadness, because the families which had lost their own houses when the Germans carried out reprisals for partisan activity had lost everything, and although they were still in their hometown, they lived like fire victims and exiles.

Lilka wasn't very pious, whereas Rafał was not practicing. Now and then I would go to the old church that stood not far from the market square, but there was never any pressure to do so, nor a feeling of impropriety, which would cast suspicion on a non-practicing person. In Opatowiec, with all its resettled persons and new arrivals, there wasn't an atmosphere of enforced custom, as was the case in the small villages, such as Chlewice or Słomka.

The only one from our circle who was both religious and practicing was Jan Pociej. At the beginning of the war, he had been an organ player and had later sung in the church choir. Usually, I would excuse myself from going to church by saying I had nothing appropriate to wear, which was true, but I did go several times with Jan. In actual fact, being in church during mass always involved some risk. I heard a story that took place in Słomka: One day a Jewish woman who had been in hiding appeared in church. During mass she behaved rather differently, not like the others, which someone noticed and reacted to, and as a result everybody learned who she really was.

Like in every other place, Opatowiec too had women of "loose virtue" who "gave" themselves to the Germans. One of them had dealings with Red Ganz and everyone knew about it. One day, in January 1945, before the Soviet occupation of the town, some local young men grabbed her, shaved her head, and inscribed, "*Nur für die Deutschen*" ("Only for the Germans") on her forehead. Then they released her so that she would suffer her humiliation among the residents of Opatowiec. Edek and Heniek also took part in this operation.

Edek was active in an underground organization and, through him, Heniek also began taking part in underground operations. I kept asking him,

"Why do you go to them? Don't you have enough problems of your own?" But he didn't listen to me. He was always an independent spirit.

In early January 1945, immediately after the New Year, a Soviet mounted patrol appeared in Nowy Korczyn. People were overcome with joy, hoping for imminent liberation, but the Soviets immediately retreated and stopped just short of Nowy Korczyn, which was about ten kilometers east of Opatowiec. The front came to a halt, but the roaring of Katyushas from which the Russians were shelling German positions was clearly heard.

Around the middle of January, the front started moving. As usual, the Russians began with a Katyusha attack along with the overwhelming roar and characteristic deafening whizz of the projectiles. The Germans who had been stationed in the area of Nowy Korczyn began a hurried evacuation and passed through Opatowiec in a disorderly fashion, heading west. On the night preceding the direct Soviet offensive, a unit of German field gendarmerie arrived at our house. They stopped and were pitching camp to eat when suddenly they heard the thunder of Soviet aircraft coming in. They sprang to their feet in panic and started fleeing; some even left their equipment behind. We, too, fled to the nearby Opatowiec forest—Rafał, Heniek, myself, the Orłowskis, Lilka and her mother, the Wiewiór family, and some other neighbors and acquaintances. We hid in the woods all night until about noon the next day.

The Russians often employed the tactic of surrounding the enemy, creating an encirclement or "cauldron," and then striking from the least expected side. This time the Germans expected the Russians to attack from the northeast, from the side where the town was surrounded by fortifications, but instead they crossed the frozen Vistula by foot. I saw a German, who was observing the Russian movements from a nearby rooftop, notice the Soviet troops' movements, and having seen them coming in from the direction of the Vistula, quickly jumped off the roof and started fleeing in panic, shouting something to his comrades.

By crossing the frozen Vistula, the Russians completely surprised the Germans, appearing suddenly on the edge of the town from the unfortified side, from which they were least expected. With lightning speed they surrounded the Germans and the Nazis panicked. Every now and then someone shouted "*Donnerwetter Iwan!*" They were fleeing without any order—some jumped out of the trenches, others were trapped by their own barbed-wire barriers and defensive fortifications, while others threw off their uniforms in order to hide among the population. The German transport formations stationed in Opatowiec, which were supposed to defend the front, withdrew without a fight. Opatowiec was liberated! We decided to return home after we heard the shooting and commotion in town die down.

"Girls," said Edek's mother, "wrap your heads with shawls and hide your faces. When the Russkies come, just hide." We returned to the house and by that time the town was filled to capacity with Soviet troops. Some were stationed by our house, having pitched camp in the yard. They looked pitiful—emaciated, unshaven, filthy, some wearing threadbare uniforms. Not all of them had shoes, only some cloth or rags wrapped around their feet. They lorded over us like victors.

They also entered the kitchen where the three of us lived. As luck would have it, Rafał had just left his wristwatch on the table, a Swiss Tissot, already without the chain, as he had sold that earlier. The Russians saw this gem, which for them was priceless, and of course, one of them took the watch without saying a word. They also, nonaggressively, searched for food and alcohol. Rafał, who knew Russian perfectly, started talking to them, asking them where they were from, about their battles, the liberated areas, and the course of the war.

The Soviet soldiers visited all the houses in town one by one. They took everything they found useful. In their search for pitiful spoils of war, they entered the pharmacy and tasted some medicines, drank concoctions and perfumes thinking they were alcohol! But they didn't tarry in Opatowiec for long. They traversed the town and moved on. All that remained was the Soviet headquarters, as in all other places, which comprised a commander with a small detachment of soldiers.

People celebrated the victory but they were also afraid, asking themselves, what was next. There was prejudice against the Soviets, as people knew that in addition to liberating us from the Nazi occupation, they were also bringing new power—their own. There were no signs of public enthusiasm for the victors. Opatowiec was tired of the war and the long occupation, the population was decimated, and besides, right-wing views dominated the town, and the freedom brought on by the Soviet bayonets did not provoke enthusiasm. The joy of liberation was marred by their fear of the future.

How did I feel after the war was over? I was relieved somewhat about the end of the torment and the constant fear that accompanied me, but I didn't experience a deep, full joy. Of my family, only Heniek and I were left and awareness of this fact brought pain and despair. The war was over and the questions I faced were: What next? What does the future hold in store for me? The war was over and the times of escape and hiding were over, but what was going to be? It was hard to say, because things were very unclear.

In February, shortly after the liberation of Opatowiec, the three of us—Rafał, Heniek and I—began talking about our next move, how to plan our next step. We had to make preparations for leaving Opatowiec where nothing held us anymore. Heniek and I wanted to get to Jędrzejów as quickly as possible, hoping against hope that perhaps we'd learn something new about our loved ones or even more distant relatives, and perhaps meet someone who had managed to survive. Perhaps we would recover some of the things we had vouchsafed in order to begin our lives anew.

For his part, Rafał wanted first to get to his native area of Rychwał and Grodziec, to meet his loved ones, to hear their stories, and to find out about the possibilities of work and living quarters. Other deportees and refugees who had been brought to Opatowiec by the fortunes of war and occupation also started leaving town, heading for their native localities or in search of a new place to live.

We started making preparations to leave. Rafał and Heniek joined forces with a Polish acquaintance of theirs and bought a pig. This Pole had ended up in Opatowiec by accident and he used to visit us, especially Rafał, together with his wife, who had very obvious Semitic features. Was she Jewish? We didn't know. Perhaps she was. But, after all, for others I, too, was Rafał's "niece," while in reality I was Heniek's niece. For many different reasons during the war, many family and personal relations lost their clarity or were disguised.

In any event, as part of our preparations for leaving Opatowiec, Heniek used the butchering skills he had learned in the course of his long apprenticeship with Wieczorek Heniek, and applied himself to making all kinds of meat cuts. He smoked kielbasa and bacon, and pickled other meat. All of us boldly helped him in these endeavors. We put aside some of the meat and the rest we ate as we worked.

Throughout his wanderings during the occupation, Rafał had managed to hold on to the suitcase he had had with him when he was expelled from Grodziec. He took his pillow, some personal items, a medical encyclopedia, and several other books. He decided to leave all his other property in his suitcase in Opatowiec in order not to be burdened too much on his journey to the unknown. He gave this suitcase for safekeeping to our neighbor, Mrs. Stankowska, who lived opposite our house, on the other side of the so-called king's road, which passed through Opatowiec from Sandomierz to Kraków. Stankowska, an older woman and very decent, once told me something that I remember to this day: "When you are successful people envy you, and when you have nothing people commiserate with you. But overall, it's better to be envied than to be commiserated with." Stankowska was a widow and had raised two daughters, Janka and Maryna. They were slightly older than I was, but we were friends; we met quite often and I visited them now and then. We also took water from their place because there was no well in Wawrzykowska's farmyard.

And so Rafał decided to leave his suitcase with Mrs. Stankowska, but this was not the end of the suitcase story. In 1946, Rafał sent his nephew Zenek from Wielkopolska to recover the suitcase. It goes without saying that Stankowska handed over the suitcase without any problem, but during Zenek's return journey it was stolen by Soviet soldiers.

Aunt Miecia, her daughter Hania and Hania's daughter Beata, Warsaw, 1980

CHAPTER 4

PICKING UP THE PIECES

THE BITTERNESS OF RETURN

We took with us the meat we had prepared earlier, as well as some *bimber*, which Lilka gave us. At that time, *bimber* was the most practical, and virtually the only means, of payment. Soviet military transports were moving on all the roads and the soldiers were willing to give a ride to civilians, but you had to pay for it, and *bimber* turned out to be irreplaceable in this regard.

The three of us reached Busko, where we stopped for the night and slept on the floor of some building. We parted the next day. Rafał was heading for his hometown, whereas Heniek and I were traveling to Jędrzejów. We parted from Rafał with assurances that we would remain in touch and that soon—nobody knew when—we would meet one another again.

Heniek and I walked towards Jędrzejów, as if against hope, fully aware that by returning to the familiar places, so dear to us, we would have to cope with the terrible tragedy of our loved ones. We were torn between the flickering hope of meeting our loved ones and acquaintances, and the fear of confronting the terrible story of the extermination of our family. We reached Jędrzejów toward evening and walked discreetly, as if hiding. We didn't want people to learn about our return right away, not knowing what situation we might find ourselves in and who we might meet. We headed straight to Aunt Miecia's, at the Leszczyński estate on the far edge of town. Miecia was tremendously relieved to learn of our survival and was astonished and delighted with our return. She assured us that she had thought about us all that time, prayed for our survival, and believed we would survive. Since my departure in March 1943, she had had no news about us—not a word for two years. After all, we couldn't have notified her about our vicissitudes, as it could have been dangerous.

Aunt Miecia greeted us with open arms, offering us lodging and food. She asked a lot of questions about Rafał, his current whereabouts, his health, and where he had gone. Maryla, Hania, and Tosia fell on me, delighted by my survival and return. They asked me to tell them the whole story, without passing over any details. It turned out that in the meantime Miecia's father, old Płakowski—the same one who had once made such a mess of things by telling Rafał that I had hid from him at the Leszczyńskis, after leaving Chlewice—had died. Aunt Miecia was worried about the prolonged pulmonary disease of her youngest daughter, Tosia. Despite attempts at curing it, the disease refused to budge.

Aunt Miecia's estate was filled with travelers—about 20 people were living there when I arrived—a sister with her husband, a niece, and distant cousins with children. Some had escaped from Warsaw after the uprising. Another family with five children sought shelter at her estate after leaving Sandomierz. The house buzzed, there was movement everywhere, but people were kind and friendly. At that time, nobody outside of the estate knew that Heniek and I had returned to Jędrzejów, but the news had spread by the second day.

We arrived in Jędrzejów empty-handed, knowing that my father had left all kinds of things with friendly Polish families for safekeeping. We also knew that Wawrzek Wesołowski had despoiled Grandfather's house and we wanted to recover what was ours, to begin life anew somehow, find lodgings, and change our clothes, so we decided that we should first pay a visit to Wesołowski.

We knew that after the deportation of my grandparents and all the other residents of the ghetto, Wesołowski, in partnership with his brother-in-law, had simply stripped bare the entire household. They had taken livestock, agricultural machinery (including a horse-driven mill, which was a rarity in those days), as well as household utensils, furniture, and cooking pots. Wesołowski's brother-in-law and his family had taken up residence in my grandparents' house, because Wesołowski himself was rich and had his own house.

We were told that as soon as they learned about our return, the Wesołowskis panicked and started hurriedly removing all kinds of things from both houses. Heniek went to see Wesołowski, demanding that he hand back the things belonging to his parents, because we had emerged from the misery of war without anything and we wanted to start our lives anew. Wesołowski promised that, yes, he would give back the "retained" items and suggested a meeting over this matter at the mayor's office.

For my part, I went to Wawrzek Wesołowski's house to meet with his wife and ask her for some kitchen utensils and plates. I entered the kitchen and saw my grandmother's Passover dinner service in the cupboard. There was no mistake: These were the same plates which had been kept in a special box in the attic, and which we used to bring down once a year, wash thoroughly, and put on the Passover table. When I asked Wesołowska whether she could give us back these plates, because for us they were a token of remembrance of Heniek's parents and my grandparents, she refused. She added that the service was not from our house, but had been bought from the Germans with *Bezugsschein* (ration cards).

Heniek fared even worse. The meeting with Wesołowski at the mayor's office did not bring any results. On the contrary, Wawrzek brought with him a policeman who started to aim his pistol at Heniek, threatening that he would kill him if he persisted with his claims. Heniek's demeanor was conciliatory. Scared by the threats, he explained that he didn't even have any other clothes to put on. Wesołowski replied that it wasn't his duty to dress Heniek and that he had bought all those things from the Germans. Heniek returned empty handed and humiliated by Wesołowski's brazenness and threats.

Wesołowski's brother-in-law, the same one who was still living in my grandparents' house and had no plans to move out, also threatened us by repeating to various acquaintances, perhaps on purpose, hoping that this threat would reach us, "They should be quiet or else we'll liquidate them."

Upset by all these developments, Heniek went to see the Soviet commander in town. He told him about the recent events and the threats against us. The commandant replied that Heniek was welcome to submit an official complaint and a testimony; they were willing to arrest Wesołowski and immediately dispatch all those involved to Siberia, but Heniek replied that he didn't want to take revenge. Other Poles also told stories about Wawrzek Wesołowski's misdeeds during the war and encouraged Heniek to make him pay for them, but Heniek replied, "Why aren't you doing it yourselves? You want people to say that the Jew took his revenge. I won't take revenge. I had things and will get them back."

However, after these events we felt threatened and therefore didn't leave the house in the evenings to go to town or simply to take a walk, because we feared that someone would attack us. So we continued living at Aunt Miecia's and spent Easter at the Leszczyński's estate, with all the cousins and other relatives who also lived there at the time. Władek Felis, the servant, was very close to us.

Following these distressing events with the Wesołowskis, I didn't want to live, or even show my face, in the part of town near my grandparents' house and the Leszczyński's estate. I felt the old fears returning, the tightness of fear and the inner tension. I didn't know how to put my life back together again. However, despite everything, I started attending school after a break of several years.

Shortly after the holidays I moved to the center of the town, where I rented a room in an outbuilding from Mrs. Mauer. Hania started attending high school, which opened immediately after the liberation of Jędrzejów, but as she found it too tiring to walk to and from school, she moved in with me at Mrs. Mauer's. We felt safer together. Marysia and Tosia Leszczyńska stayed at the estate with their mother. Sadly, Tosia, who had been ill and was wasting away, died shortly after that, but already after my departure.

For his part, Heniek began traveling to various places in Poland, particularly Zagłębie (the coal basin) and the recently recovered western lands, in the search for acquaintances, contacts, work opportunities, and living quarters. He kept returning to Jędrzejów, making brief stops at Aunt Miecia's or to visit some acquaintances of his before hitting the road again. I wrote to Rafał at the address in Rychwał, saying I was in Jędrzejów, and gave him my address. He replied almost immediately and continued writing letters.

After I returned to Jędrzejów, I didn't meet with Tola right away. Ever since I had left Jędrzejów and its environs, I hadn't been in touch with her. I learned about her war experiences only after my return. At that time, Tola was still living with her four brothers: Julek, Józek, Lutek, and Miecio. She was in charge of the household, while her brothers were busy with the farm. From what Rafał told me, I knew that during the war Tola had sheltered an entire Jewish family from Sędziszów. The successive chapters of this story were recounted to me by some acquaintances, Aunt Miecia, and Tola herself.

One day, Tola was caught in the Nazi dragnet that took place in Jędrzejów. She was expected to be taken away to Germany for forced labor, but Julek volunteered to take her place and he went instead of her. We heard about this while we were living in Słomka, because Heniek was using papers issued in the name of Julek Grzywnowicz.

Tola stayed behind with her three remaining brothers and continued sheltering the Jewish family: a mother with four children. The oldest of the children was 20 years old, two of the sisters were teenagers, and the youngest boy was nine years old. During the day they stayed in a special hideout, where they also slept during the night, but in the evenings they often went to the Grzywnowicz's house and spent time with the siblings. On one occasion, Rafał encountered all of them and thought that this arrangement wasn't safe. The Grzywnowicz's house was located outside of town on an extensive, isolated farmyard, concealed from behind by an orchard and in the front by trees and brushwood; nonetheless, five people hiding there could not remain a secret for long, especially since the family had been residing in the house for a long time.

One night, in 1943, a group of Poles, possibly belonging to some organization, entered Tola's house. She recognized some of them as well as their commander, named Gajos. They explained they had come for the hiding Jews. After Tola tried to resist and defend the hiding family, they put a pistol to her head and told her to be quiet. The bandits brought the entire family of five people from their hiding place but, due to the darkness and the commotion, the oldest of the siblings managed to slip away and hide in the utility buildings. The bandits thought he had fled to the fields and didn't pursue him. They took the mother and her three other children to the woods near Skroniów, left them there, and notified the Germans that a Jewish family had been found. So while they didn't shoot them themselves, they did arrange their murder with the Nazis, who arrived at the site immediately and finished the savage deed themselves.

Meanwhile, as the bandits were escorting the captured Jews through the fields, the escaped son managed to notify Tola that he had survived and was in the farmyard. Tola then escaped with him right away, as she was afraid of further reprisals. Tola's three brothers stayed put and the next day the policeman Marecki came and warned them that the Germans would probably come for them also. The boys decided not to flee. Perhaps they didn't take the warning to heart, or perhaps they thought that the Nazis wouldn't investigate the matter further. Besides, they had livestock in the farmyard, which they needed to look after. Nonetheless, during the first days after the incident, they stayed away from the house and only returned at night to guard the house and feed the livestock. However, their caution proved ineffective and after some time the Germans came for the boys, who happened to be in the house at the time. Józek and Lutek were arrested, brought to Jędrzejów and executed. Józek was 23 and Lutek was 21 at the time. The Germans left Miecio alone, perhaps because of his young age. Immediately after this tragedy, Tola came to take Miecio to Chorzewa, to live with her husband, who worked as a forester. The house remained empty.

Until the end of the war Tola continued to hide with the escaped son. They stayed in some village in the Kielce region, in the house of a Polish woman. Tola lived "outside," among the people, whereas the young Jew lived in a hideout underneath the floor. Despite some difficult moments, throughout this time Tola helped the young man and took care of him. On one occasion the Germans charged the house in search of hiding partisans. The entrance to the hiding place underneath the floor was covered by a bed and luckily the Nazis did not discover it. Tola and the young man succeeded in surviving the inferno of the occupation and after liberation the young Jew discovered two cousins who had survived the war in a camp.

Shortly after liberation, this young Jew decided to travel to his native Sędziszów, to recover the things that had been left with Polish families for safekeeping. Tola and his two cousins tried to dissuade him, explaining that it was still too dangerous, asking him to wait a bit longer with his expedition. However, he refused to listen to their pleas, mounted a bicycle and vanished off the face of the earth. Inquiries and further searches brought no result. He must have died, perhaps by accident or during an attack by bandits, although there were also certainly incidents in which Jews were killed just because they had returned to claim their property, or had survived thus far.

Together with the two cousins of the missing young Jew, Tola returned to Jędrzejów, still awaiting the return of her friend or at least some news about him. She couldn't go back to her own house, because other residents had taken it over. She felt terribly lonely and crushed by her war experiences.

One day in Jędrzejów, Tola ran into Gajos, the leader of the gang that had taken away the Jewish family from her house.

"You were there!" she screamed, even though she was very frightened.

"So what? You pity Jews? Do you have witnesses by any chance?" he replied with haughtiness.

"They were human beings and my brothers were also killed because of you," Tola sobbed.

But there was nothing she could do in the postwar disorder. Besides, she was afraid for herself. One day someone shot at her in the center of Jędrzejów and she barely managed to hide behind the gate of some house. Where could she look for justice? Later Gajos disappeared and apparently stayed in hiding for some time.

Shortly after the end of the war, Julek, who had been in Germany as a forced laborer, returned, emaciated, to Jędrzejów. Miecio was living with his eldest sister in Chorzewa. The three of them, Julek, Tola, and Miecio, all carried the wounds of their family's tragedy. They returned to their house, but sold it shortly thereafter.

The two cousins of the young Jew who had gone missing left Poland shortly thereafter and emigrated to Australia. One of them, Regina, married one of the Kluski brothers, who had survived by hiding with a Polish family in Jędrzejów.

My father, who had kept a textile store, had had many friendly clients. Among them was a Polish couple—a railroad worker and his wife. They often borrowed money from my father and he never refused them. They had two children: a daughter, Klara, who was a teacher; and a son who briefly attended Catholic seminary.

During the war, when the Jędrzejów ghetto still existed but we were still living with my grandparents, who had also taken in my father with his new family, Father went to this friendly family and gave them his fur coat and textile samples for safekeeping. He told me about it as if he had known that only I would survive, "Rózia, you might be left alone. Remember to whom I gave the fur coat and textiles for safekeeping. You'll be able to get them back." So I went to see this family. They recognized me, of course, and I asked them about Father's fur coat. Father used to wear it only once in a while, on the High Holidays. It was completely new, covered with black fabric, lined with fur, and with a black fur collar. In reply to my enquiry, Klara said that the Soviets had come and taken it. But other people told me they had seen Klara wearing the coat, which had been altered to fit her.

"OK," I said, not wanting to argue, "but I need something to wear, some clothes. I just came back and the only thing I have is this dress."

"Oh," they replied, "the Russkies came and turned the house upside down. The fur coat and clothes were in the attic, and they took them all."

They didn't return anything, nor did they help me with anything.

I also went to see another of Father's acquaintances, who I also knew from before the war. They were known as a decent family and Father must have trusted them if he had given them our things for safekeeping. I remember that, prior to our deportation to the ghetto, these people transferred lengths of cloth and pieces of fabric from my grandparents' house to their house. So I went to see them, to ask them to return the materials that were given to them for safekeeping.

"Times were hard, there was poverty, we used these fabrics to make clothes for ourselves and to sell, just to survive," they said.

"I understand," I replied, "but perhaps something is left? Help me, I really don't have anything," I asked them nicely, politely. What did it mean, nothing was left?

"Perhaps we'll find something, some leftovers. Come back later, in a few days," they replied.

They seemed troubled and embarrassed. When I came to them a second time, they said they had nothing and hadn't found anything. They gave me some food, a pat of butter, and that was all. No clothing whatsoever, not a penny.

All those whom I asked for help or to return the items that had been vouchsafed to them behaved in the same fashion; everybody except Aunt Leszczyńska.

Grandmother had left with Aunt Leszczyńska a festive tablecloth and two very beautiful and expensive bedspreads, which had been bought in Kraków and were part of my mother's wedding trousseau, which she had kept for me for after her death. They were made of a specially woven cloth, hand painted with vivid flowers on a dark background. Aunt Leszczyńska had kept everything that Grandmother vouchsafed to her, and she gave them back to me immediately after my return. She said, "Now these are treasures, as a remembrance of your dear mother, and your beloved grandparents. They were always wonderful to me. Keep those things with care."

There were very upright and noble-minded people, but there were others who were dishonorable and greedy. I learned that even after the war, after my return to Jędrzejów, human greed knows no bounds; it can lead to lawlessness and even to crime.

I encountered hostility, which stemmed only from the fact that I had survived. For example, Krysia, the daughter of the infamous Wawrzek Wesołowska, who despoiled my grandparents' house, sent Heniek and me away empty-handed and even threatened us. She had been my classmate before the war and when she found out that I had survived and returned to Jędrzejów, she allegedly said to our mutual friend, Adela Olszewska (who repeated her words to me), "How come? Everybody was murdered and she alone survived?" Deeply moved by these words, I kept asking myself who gave her the right to speak that way? Did she value her life differently? Or the life of her father, who looted my grandparents' house and then drove us away?

The handful of Holocaust survivors from Jędrzejów returned to their homes, each and every one of them carrying the burden of the tragic memory of their loved and dear ones who had been murdered by the Nazis, the burden of their dramatic escapes, and constant hiding and living in fear.

Very seldom did someone manage to remain in hiding successfully until the end of the war. However, some did manage this feat. Two Jewish brothers by the name of Kluski, who originated from Jędrzejów, had hidden out in the attic of the house of a Polish family, with the family's help, of course. They survived and now live in Australia. I met the younger brother, Henryk, 38 years after the war in Abano, Italy. The older brother's name was Itzek Majer.

A woman from Jędrzejów named Mauer, who now lives in Israel, was in hiding with her daughter. Because both of them had blond hair, it was fairly simple to arrange Aryan papers for them, and they traveled to Warsaw as it was easier to hide in a big city. A Pole took care of them. Mauer's husband was hidden by a Polish family in Jędrzejów and all of them survived in this fashion. After the war, the mother and daughter returned to Jędrzejów and later, all of them immigrated to Israel.

Our cousin on my grandfather's side, Perla-Pola Fajgenblat, also survived and returned to Jędrzejów. Before the war and in the first years of the occupation her parents had operated a bakery. After the Germans expelled all of us to the ghetto, we lived in their house together with my grandparents. Her husband, Abram Frucht, perished in the camp. After her return and with the help of a family member who also survived the death camp, Pola revived the bakery. Eventually she immigrated to Australia, where she lives to this day.

Another two survivors were Śledzik and his 18-year-old son. Before the war, Śledzik had owned a fur store and he also did not manage to recover the furs and fabrics that he had given to acquaintances for safekeeping. Śledzik was attacked and shot at through a window. He was shot in the larynx and only survived by a miracle. Later, he was fitted with an artificial larynx. Needless to say, the perpetrators were not found.

My grandfather, Mechel Landschaft, had nine siblings. From this large family, entire branches of several generations perished in the Holocaust. Luckily—if that is the word to use under such circumstances—nine people from Mechel's family survived, including one of his children: Heniek; Pola Fajgenblat, daughter of his sister Hendla; Aron Majer Landschaft; Kopel Landschaft; and Shmuel Czałczyński, son of his sister Perla.

The story of Shmuel's survival was both dramatic and strange. He was born in Włoszczowa in 1915, finished cobbler's school, and worked in his profession. He continued to live in Włoszczowa and remained single until the war broke out. When the Germans began liquidating the ghetto in Włoszczowa, in September 1942, Shmuel and 15 other young Jews fled to the woods. They had already been in touch prior to that with a local unit of the Home Army (AK). They were supposed to receive weapons from Polish partisans and organize themselves into a Jewish armed unit. However, the partisans failed to show up for the agreed meeting; someone had passed the information on to the Germans. Instead, a Nazi unit from Włoszczowa prepared a manhunt. The Jewish escapees had only two grenades, which they lobbed in the direction of the Germans and the Nazis responded with automatic weapons. Fifteen Jews were killed in the massacre, with only Shmuel surviving. Having been wounded by six bullets, he fell among the other bodies and the Germans concluded that he was dead. Shmuel somehow managed to drag himself to a Polish farm owned by a man named Mularczyk. He was taken in, his wounds were bandaged, and he was given a bed for the night. They were afraid to shelter him for longer because they had four children, but the next day they took him to Mularczyk's father, who lived with his other son and daughter-in-law. Shmuel had money with him and at first, the elder Mularczyk refused to accept it, but after Shmuel insisted, Mularczyk agreed that he could pay him for shelter and upkeep.

One night, Shmuel awoke from an extraordinary dream. In the dream he saw his mother, who said to him, "Son, you are asleep here, while they want to kill you." When he awoke he overheard his landlords talking about him, making plans to take him to the woods and kill him there. He confronted them immediately and they were frightened by his sudden appearance. He said to them with conviction that he had slipped away from death once and he wouldn't let it happen a second time. If something were to happen to him, he warned them, they too would perish. He stayed with them and they sheltered him until the end of the war.

After liberation Shmuel arrived for a brief period in Jędrzejów, where we met. He told me that immediately after the war, he had returned to Włoszczowa and buried in a mass grave his 15 comrades, who had perished tragically as a result of betrayal, and had put up a tombstone. Then he left for Wrocław and from there to Paris.

The entire Fajgenblat family also survived; they had hidden for several years in a dug-out trench on a Chlewice farm, under the care of a Polish family named Loti. Another two cousins of mine on Grandfather Mechel's side survived Auschwitz: Bronia Nowytargiel, nee Frucht, who lives in Israel; and Roza Wechadłowska.

Of the several thousand Jews who had lived in Jędrzejów and the environs, only a few more than ten survived. Each of them survived in a different fashion, each in dramatic circumstances. The wounds of their tragic personal experiences have never healed, pulsing with memories evoked both in subconsciousness and consciousness. These wounds were often reopened by the remembrance of unpleasant and humiliating experiences of the postwar years, and later by other difficult events.

I also learned how my other grandfather, Fajwisz Chęciński from Wodzisław, died. When the Nazis were expelling the Wodzisław Jews from their houses in order to transport them to the camp for certain death, my grandfather refused to leave his house and was shot right then and there, in the entrance to his house.

In Jędrzejów, I also had to get my formal and civilian issues in order. I emerged from the war with a *kenkarte* issued in the name of Stańisława

Kaczmarek. After returning to Jędrzejów, I began proceedings to have my name changed again. My birth certificate had been preserved in the municipal registry and based on that I returned to my true name—Chęcińska. The only remaining problem was my first name. The name on my birth certificate was Ruchla, but I never used it. At home I was called Rózia and even school certificates referred to me as Rozalia. But for now, my old name had to remain. I received an identity document issued in the name of Ruchla Chęcińska.

Rafał sent letters regularly, describing his own vicissitudes. He stressed that he missed me, wanted to see me, and was waiting for me to come see him as soon as possible. He had to return to his hometown in order to find his dear ones or learn about their fate and regarded our separation as temporary. Rafał was absolutely convinced we would meet again and later get married. He did not present me with any demands or limitations, leaving me free to do as I pleased, but he kept assuring me that he had remained faithful to the feelings he had been harboring towards me for a long time. How certain was he that we would get married? Well, there was no doubt as far as he was concerned; he emerged from all trials and adversities further strengthened in his conviction that he wanted to marry me.

I replied to his letters and described to him the situation in Jędrzejów: who we met and what events took place. "I have not yet regained my balance," I wrote, "and have found little peace since the inferno of the experiences of the war, which remain fresh." The fear and sense of being endangered, returned. The questions of how to build a future for myself remained open.

Rafał empathized with my situation, my experiences, and my state of mind (after all, he had gotten to know me very well in those years of shared, difficult experiences), and encouraged me to visit him. He had no plans to remain in Rychwał or in Grodziec, but intended to move to the western territories. Needless to say, I was in a state of confusion. I spoke with Aunt Miecia, asking her what to do. How to live now? Where? With whom? We had been very close for many years. As she herself had told me many times, she treated me like her fourth daughter. Throughout the war years, she became even closer to me through her dedication and the sacrifices she made for me. She was almost like my mother. She knew my story and respected my indecision. I didn't keep any secrets from her and she understood my need to begin life anew, but certainly not in Jędrzejów—that was as clear to her as it was to me—where so many people greeted Heniek and me with animosity and even hostility.

Aunt Miecia was also aware of Rafał's feelings and intentions toward me; she also knew very well all that Rafał had done for me and Heniek, and that he had risked his life to rescue us both. "I helped you just a little bit," she said to me, "but you owe your survival to him above all."

While respecting my right to choose and make decisions about my life, Aunt Miecia nonetheless advised me—because I asked her to—to visit Rafał and see what the future might bring. Throughout the occupation years she had gotten to know Rafał very well and had witnessed his attachment to me. She was convinced that he would care for me, be kind to me, and be my trusted and dedicated life companion.

I decided to go, without making any decisions about anything. I also wanted to leave Jędrzejów behind me, the place of my childhood, my tragedy, bitterness, and a remembrance of my most cruel experiences.

ANEW AGAIN

It was late summer 1945 and I traveled by train from Jędrzejów to Konin, and from there by bus to Rychwał. Rafał and I met after several months of separation, which had been full of difficult experiences. Rafał was overjoyed by my arrival. He didn't plan to remain in his native area and was seeking work and living quarters in the western territories.

My meeting with Rafał seemed to me a kind of beginning of the next chapter of the story that we had begun together and gone through during those difficult years. Throughout this period of escape, hiding, shared dangers, and finally, survival, I had become attached to him. He was close to me through the bond of shared experiences. He was also close because of his care and sacrifice for my sake and because he had risked his life for me.

Heniek wasn't in Jędrzejów when I left. He was on yet another of his travels to Silesia and the western territories, searching for acquaintances, contacts, work, and an apartment. When he returned to Jędrzejów, he was told about my destination and some time later, he arrived in Rychwał to visit Rafał and me. He said he was getting settled in Wrocław and told us how he happened to meet up in Kalisz with Tarczyński, who had sheltered me for a while in Łąkta Górna. Heniek showed his gratitude to Tarczyński by giving him a sum of money.

I stayed in Rychwał for almost three weeks. My situation and life prospects kept changing, but at the same time also assumed some form. My social and private life became frenzied in those first months after the war, as if people wanted to make up for the lost war years. I began thinking seriously about staying with Rafał for good and remaining in Poland.

In the meantime, Rafał had found work in Legnica, at the Education Inspectorate. He had already transferred some of his belongings there and I was supposed to join him soon thereafter. I traveled to Legnica in the company of two of Rafał's former students, now adults, for whom he had managed to find work in the local schools. We traveled via Poznań, taking with us parcels and boxes containing Rafał's belongings and mine, including bedding and food—mostly flour and fruit preserves. The trains and railroad stations were incredibly congested and messy and in all the commotion, our food package was stolen by Soviet soldiers.

Our stint in Legnica turned out to be very brief, as the Education Inspectorate where Rafał worked in the reorganization of schools in the western territories, was moved to Wrocław, so we moved there too. We settled in Wrocław in the fall of 1945 and an apartment was assigned to us. Heniek had settled in Wrocław some time earlier and I immediately contacted him. Our cousins, Pola Fajgenblat, Shmuel Czałczyński, and Aron Majer Landschaft, also lived there, and Maryla and Hania Leszczyński ended up there too. Maryla started medical school, whereas Hania had to pass the matriculation exam first. She then began courses in mathematics and natural studies, which she later discontinued in order to enroll in nursing school. The Wieczorek family, with whom we had stayed in Słomka, came to Wrocław several times. Out of gratitude for his help during the war years, Heniek gave them financial support. One day Wieczorek came to Wrocław in the company of a young Jew, Abram Lipinowski from Grodziec. Abram met Pola Fajgenblat, they liked each other, and married soon thereafter.

Similar to many other Polish Jews, including our relatives and acquaintances, Heniek did not plan to remain in Poland and they were all busy making preparations to leave. They also tried to talk me into leaving with them, but I stuck to my decision to remain in Poland.

In the fall of 1946 this entire group, with whom we had remained in touch during our life in Wrocław, left Poland. First, they traveled to Germany and then each went in different directions: Heniek and Shmuel Czałczyński to

Paris, Aron Majer Landschaft to Israel, and the Lipinowski couple, Pola and Abram, to Australia.

Shortly after my arrival in Wrocław I began studying, first by correspondence and then by attending evening classes at the commercial and trade school. I also began studying piano at a music school and continued my musical education for four years. Throughout this time, I also worked.

In Wrocław, the question of my original name came up again. I never used my given first name, both because I didn't like it and because it immediately revealed my origins: "Ruchla—she must be Jewish." My last name, Chęcińska, sounded very Polish and everything was "spoiled" by my given name. I didn't want people to know right away who I was—at home, at work, in school. I feared being "exposed." My reluctance to "reveal" myself had to do with the trauma of my war experiences, as well as the situation in Poland in the early postwar years, when the dislike of Jews was flaunted openly and bluntly in different situations and in many places. My life passed in the shadow of the fear of being exposed, of being who I was, and in the complexity of being someone else and a stranger to others. In view of all this, I wanted to change my given name. Many Polish Jews who survived the Holocaust behaved similarly.

Together with Rafał, I looked for another name. The first choice was Sabina, which both of us liked. I had to change my name officially through the Office of Civilian Status and then in all the documents and places with which I was formally connected. So I formally became Sabina Chęcińska, until Rafał and I married in October 1947. I assumed his name and since then I have been Sabina Kałowska. However, many of my acquaintances still address me as Dzidka.

Changing my name into a Polish-sounding one brought some comfort in everyday life. At school or work, whenever my personal details were required, people knew who I was—Sabina Kałowska, daughter of Aron and Chana—but it certainly did not solve the problem. On the contrary, it made my heritage obvious and added to the prevailing feeling of unease.

Like many other Polish Jews, especially those who had spent the war hiding on the Aryan side, I experienced a "necessity" to cover up my identity, my true face, and history, like someone who tries to avoid being slapped. This was easiest done at work. I told Rafał about various instances of unpleasantness I had encountered and he, who experienced these incidents as painfully as I did, was upset, but there was nothing he could do. All my wartime experiences had not healed and the pain of "exposure" was felt once again. This was the reason for my making efforts to remain in the shadows, to keep my distance toward people so that I wouldn't be noticed. I was mistrustful, tense, and fearful of "exposure" at all times.

Echoes of the wartime events and the tragic fate of the Polish Jews kept returning. In 1947, a trial took place in Kielce in connection with the murder of the Jewish Miedziński family, who had lived on the outskirts of Jędrzejów. This macabre mass murder had become well known. The trial reverberated loudly throughout Jędrzejów and its environs. The defendants were more than a dozen identified participants in the savage "operation" who, under the leadership of Mróz, took part, to various degrees, in the hunt for the Miedzińskis and in the crime itself.

It is possible that I wouldn't have known anything about all this if I hadn't received a letter from the son of the farmer Łukos, whose father had taken part in the manhunt and had been accused together with the others.

In his letter, the young Łukos pleaded with me to come to Kielce as a witness for the defense of his father. He stressed that his father had been coerced by the leaders of this operation to take part in the manhunt and was a participant only out of fear and worry for his family. Łukos reminded me that his father had been well known by Grandfather Mechel and that the two had maintained good neighborly relations. He added that I was the only person who could attest to this, and that my opinion could help his father.

Old Łukos had done occasional work for my grandfather, bringing firewood and helping with farmyard work. He visited my grandparents quite often, sat with Grandfather to talk, poked fun at me, and I at him. He also used to stop by during the war. Grandfather never said a bad word about him and I, too, remembered Łukos as a good person.

Owing to the sense of decency and uprightness that Grandfather had instilled in us, himself being a good example, I thought I should help in this matter and agreed to take part in the proceedings as a character witness for the defense of Łukos. I traveled from Wrocław to Kielce at my own expense in order to be in court on the appointed date. I testified for Łukos's sake, in accordance with what I knew about him and to the extent that I knew him. The court took my testimony into account and during sentencing, the judge mentioned my positive opinion of the defendant and that it had been taken into consideration. Łukos received the most lenient punishment of all the participants and his son expressed his heartfelt thanks to me for my willingness to help. I was of the opinion that the truth was worth more than personal resentment.

This case, once again, opened before me the depth of tragedy that struck the Miedzińskis, as well as my loved ones, and the drama of my own experiences. I was astonished to discover that among the witnesses was Wawrzek Wesołowski. His presence shook me to my core. I told some people there that he should be on the other side, together with the defendants, and appealed to the court to prevent Wesołowski from giving testimony. Many of those who took part in the hunt for the Jewish family and the gruesome murder were sentenced to imprisonment.

The postwar "score-settling" affected Rafał in a different fashion. One evening in March 1947, security functionaries came to our apartment and arrested Rafał for political reasons. The whole case went back to the years of occupation in Grodziec and, as was usually the case, was convoluted and complicated. A man named Marian, Rafał's former student, an irresponsible and not serious person who suffered from megalomania, lived in Grodziec. During the occupation he pretended he was German, but nobody knew why. He frightened people, blackmailed them, and boasted of his alleged power. At the end of the war, some partisans broke into Marian's apartment and gave him a solid beating. They extended the same treatment to other residents of Grodziec who had behaved similarly and collaborated with the Germans. Among the partisans was Edward, another of Rafał's former students, whose father had been deported by the Germans to the Dachau camp.

After the war, Marian was one of the first to volunteer for UB (Public Security) and began working as the agency's functionary. In retaliation for the beating he had suffered from the partisans, he falsely accused Edward of treason and Edward was arrested and put in prison. He was questioned and tortured. At that time, Edward's younger siblings—a brother aged 14 and a sister aged 16—were living with us in Wrocław and the UB tried to exploit this fact to hatch a plot. They presented Edward with an alleged testimony from Rafał, wherein Rafał supposedly said (even though they had not spoken with him at the time) that he had seen a firearm at Edward's. At that time, illegal possession of firearms was punishable by a long stint in prison. Edward, believing these statements—which were obviously false, but at his wits' end from all the torture and scared by the prospect of further sentencing and punishment—said that he had also seen a firearm held by Rafał. Then the security people, who received the order to arrest Rafał, swung into action. In the evening we heard loud knocking on the door. "Who is it?" Rafał asked.

"Militia, open up!" someone shouted on the other side.

I didn't let Rafał open the door. I grasped his hand, saying that this must be a trap, because the police have nothing on us. We heard the order to surround the house. Rafał opened the door, of course, and they burst in, several of them, all UB. They started turning the entire apartment upside-down, sniffing every corner in search of firearms. I got furious and started screaming, "You are exactly like the Gestapo! Have you no shame? You behave like bandits and brutes! What do you want?!"

"Be quiet or else we'll arrest you too!" they shouted back at me.

"I am not scared of you, I've been scared enough already," I replied angrily.

It goes without saying that they didn't find any firearms. Nonetheless, they arrested Rafał and Edward's brother and sister, who were still almost children.

At that time, Heniek was already in Paris. I telephoned him the next morning, telling him about the events and asking for his help. Heniek went to the Polish embassy in Paris and intervened on Rafał's behalf. I went to the police headquarters to see for myself how things stood and, albeit with great difficulty, I received a permit to see Rafał. He looked haggard, unshaven, and sleep-deprived. They summoned me for questioning.

"Where is the firearm that Mr. Kałowski has hidden? Where is his pistol? If you tell us, we'll release him."

"It wasn't a pistol! It was a machine gun! You didn't find it and now what are you going to do to us?!" I replied sarcastically.

I wasn't afraid of them at all. I was without fear, just as I had been on many similar occasions during the war, when I was in hiding and found myself in situations without any way out; or in Opatowiec, when the Germans found me next to the *bimber* production equipment. And now I was on the offensive.

"I'll kill you with my own bare hands if something happens to Rafał!" I screamed.

They asked about Heniek, knowing that he was already in Paris. They wanted his letters. I searched for something that I could throw at them, but found nothing suitable. Upset, I threw my handbag at one of them. Another one, who was already very angry, barked at me, "Be quiet this instant, or else we'll arrest you too!"

"Be my guest," I replied. "I am not afraid. I am familiar with very serious fears."

They didn't do anything to me. They finished the questioning without any results and let me go, but I was tormented over the possible consequences for Rafał. They released him after a week and the entire incident had no further consequences for Rafał. Sometime later, they also released Edward. However, having suffered numerous rounds of beatings and torture, he did not recover and died soon thereafter, at the tender age of 25.

In Wrocław I worked, among other places, in the financial and bookkeeping departments of state enterprises and it was there that I befriended Władzia. We talked a lot about many personal issues and everyday life. She too carried heavy baggage from her war experiences. I felt she harbored certain prejudices against Jews, because of the ordeals her family had suffered in Soviet Russia at the hands of the NKVD (People's Commission of Internal Affairs), which employed Jewish communists. She asked about my life and about my war experiences and was intrigued by my marriage to Rafał, asking about the reason for such a considerable age difference between us. Despite a certain intimacy between us, I replied evasively and perfunctorily. However, one day I had had enough. "Listen, Władzia," I said, "I can't go on like this anymore. You know, I have been living with half-truths. I have to tell you something. If afterwards you want to remain my friend, that is for you to decide."

"What happened, Dzidka?" Władzia was disoriented and embarrassed.

"I am Jewish. You didn't know that? You didn't suspect?"

"No," she said, "I didn't. But once, the legal advisor asked me whether Mrs. Sabina's husband was also Jewish. 'Why are you asking?' I said. 'After all, she is not Jewish.' At that time I didn't quite understand the drift of his question and didn't guess why he was asking me."

It has to be said that the legal advisor was discreet enough not to say anything more, even though, having had access to the personnel files, he must have known who I really was. I continued my conversation with Władzia. "Władzia, you don't have to be my friend anymore, but I couldn't carry on concealing the truth from you and lying to myself. Throughout all that time I wasn't myself, not with you and not with myself. This is what my conscience tells me. But since we've become so close, I felt the need and necessity to tell you the truth about myself."

My confession didn't change my relations with her. On the contrary, we remained as close as ever. After her war experiences and tragic dramas, Władzia was an orphan and had nobody in Wrocław. I had been and remained her closest friend. When she got married, I lent her my blouse for the ceremony and helped her with the reception.

For the most part, my co-workers didn't know who I was, and I tried to erase the traces that could lead to the truth. I still carried within me the old, familiar fear of this or that person discovering my origin. I was liked at work, had many colleagues and close girlfriends. But after a while, when people started whispering secretly about who I was, I felt that the atmosphere around me was changing. Some started responding coolly toward me, keeping their distance. Another distancing factor was that Poland was under communist rule by this time and I wasn't a Communist Party member. I carried a grudge against communism, especially because of the fate met by my uncle Aron Majer, who had vanished in the east without a trace. I also shared Rafał's critical views of the regime we lived under. Even though I wasn't a political person, I took part in conversations at work about the difficulties of life, about shortages, and the absurdities of the system that we happened to live under.

In Wrocław we lived very modestly, supported by a teacher's small salary and my modest earnings. We couldn't afford meat even once a week or the early seasons' fruit or vegetables. At the end of the month we could never make ends meet and I always had to borrow money from my girlfriends or neighbors, which I had difficultly repaying. In 1948, Rafał's brother Adam died. After the war Adam and his family had returned from Rabka, where they had lived for the past few years, to Poznań. It goes without saying that their house in Poznań had been commandeered by the Polish socialist state, so they took up residence there as tenants, in two rooms with a kitchen; later a subtenant moved in. Adam's wife worked as house manager. Adam had been ill for a long time and Rafał visited him quite often to help his brother in any way he could.

For the first few years in Wrocław, Rafał worked at the school's superintendent office as a department director. Gradually, the situation and the pressure of the mendacious indoctrination of the education system became intolerable for him, so he left the superintendent's office and started working as a high school teacher, hoping that at least contact with youth might allow him to remain faithful to his worldview.

All the curricula called for the teaching of Marxism and Communism, which were optimistically formulated. Rafał couldn't stand this speciousness. He used to bring home books about Marxism, bound in red cloth, and angrily ask me to read them to him, because he simply couldn't do it on his own. I would reply that I was overwhelmed by household chores and school commitments and that I couldn't—or even that I wouldn't. With his heart in his mouth, Rafał taught his students the obligatory material about Marxism. He did so by quoting things he wanted nothing to do with: Dear students, on this or that issue, the book says so and so…

Rafał was already 60 by this time and decided to take early retirement. We also started thinking about moving from Wrocław to central Poland. In Wrocław we felt like strangers, with no relatives at all and very few friends. We planned to move to Poznań or Łódź, where Rafał had relatives and because he felt an attachment to these two cities.

Rafał started making efforts in this direction in 1954. At that time, I was already pregnant and I began to experience health problems that I couldn't cope with due to our financial situation, which hadn't improved at all. My legs swelled, but we didn't have money to buy suitable shoes. My female colleagues at work noticed my situation and loaned me money to buy shoes. I also couldn't afford to buy nutritious food or vitamins. I would return from work very tired and looked with great hunger at tomatoes I couldn't afford to buy.

At the end of summer 1954, my only cousins who still remained in Poland, the Białokamińskis, invited me to stay with them in Sosnowiec. They were sincerely concerned about the state of my health and the conditions in which we lived in Wrocław. I stayed there for several weeks and it was there, in Sosnowiec, that I gave birth to my son, Tomasz, in October 1954. I spent the next six weeks with them.

Meanwhile, Rafał finished all the registration matters and other formalities related to changing one's address and moved from Wrocław to Łódź. I arrived there shortly thereafter with our little son. It was the end of 1954.

It can be said that our situation went from bad to worse. Our living conditions in Łódź were even worse than those in Wrocław. Just as in Wrocław there was only cold water in the kitchen sink; the oven worked very badly, smoked, and gave off very little heat; there was no bathroom, and the restroom was outside and was used by several dozen tenants. Furthermore, the apartment was smaller, darker, and located in an area with a lot of smoke.

The everyday life of raising an infant without any help, in yet another new location and environment, in very difficult living conditions, was a nightmare for me. Although retired, Rafał resumed his work as a teacher in various schools and was paid per hour.

Tomasz grew up in these very dire conditions, requiring constant care, medical advice, and a change of climate. When he was eight months old, he fell seriously ill with bronchitis. I was desperate and it was Hania Leszczyńska who came to the rescue. She was already a certified nurse and lived and worked in Ustronie Śląskie in the Beskidy mountains. Hania invited us to stay at her place so that Tomasz could regain his health and get strengthened by the mountain air. So I set out for the mountains together with the baby, even though I was ill and weak myself. We traveled from Łódź to Katowice by train. I was so weakened by my illness and so tired after the difficult journey that I fainted in the waiting room for mothers with small children at Katowice station. But somehow I managed to get to Ustronie. Hania greeted us with great warmth and gave us her small apartment and food, because I was literally penniless. I spent five weeks in Ustronie together with Tomasz. The fresh mountain air, suitable climate, and wholesome country food helped to restore our health and strength. In the course of our walks and conversations, Hania and I returned many times to our shared memories of Jędrzejów and our war experiences, which bound us in friendship despite the tragic events.

We—by that I mean Rafał and I—started looking again for a new place to live. We considered Poznań in Warsaw where Aunt Miecia Leszczyńska, who was always dear to me and treated me with loving care, had been living for quite a while. At about the same time, I received a modest amount of money from the sale of my Landschaft grandparents' house and field. The Białokamińskis also came to our aid and somehow we managed to gather enough money to buy a little cottage near Łódź, in Rejmontów. It had two rooms, a kitchen in a wooden annex, an entrance hall, a well in the yard, and a small garden.

We lived there for several years, but the living conditions were again terrible. The cottage was cold, without a basement, and damp. The kitchen was smoky and on one occasion I became asphyxiated, only to be saved by neighbors and the arrival of an ambulance. After Tomasz was born I didn't return to work as caring for and bringing up our son, the rigors of everyday family life, as well as the need to give Rafał moral support, filled my time completely. Life in Rejmontów lacked any prospects for the future and renovation of the cottage didn't make sense.

All those successive changes in living quarters also had a deeper context. I still carried the unhealed wound of my war experiences, which amounted not only to fleeing from the Germans, betrayal or denunciation, but also seemed to tell me to run away from myself, from my identity, to live in a corner somewhere, unnoticed.

Who am I? Where do I come from? Sooner or later the truth would surface, arousing my anxiety, my inner fears, and my readiness to flee again and change our living place—Jędrzejów, Wrocław, Łódź, further and further away… from myself and from others; at work there was my personal file; in our neighborhood the neighbors seemed to have special lenses on their eyes; when buying a house it was the personal details again. And then there were the letters to and from Israel—the sender's address gave away our "little secret" of Jewish connection and could potentially be to our disadvantage. The old times returned in Rejmontów—during playtime the neighborhood children picked on Tomasz because of his origins, something that a three- or four-year-old could not, of course, understand. However, we, his parents, did understand. We also saw the pebbles that the children threw at him together with "suitable" remarks. Rafał was very upset and threatened them.

"What do you expect and what can you do?" I tried to persuade him. This is not the children's fault, but that of the adults, the parents.

I started corresponding with my cousin who lived in Holon, in Israel. Whenever the mailman brought a letter from her, I had to sign a receipt and while doing so I went red in the face. I experienced such incidents (so prosaic for anybody else) thinking that this mailman already knew who I was. For a very long time I didn't reply to her because I didn't want to receive a letter which would, yet again, "expose" me and reveal, so I thought, who I was.

I experienced such situations as if something could still put me in danger. It is difficult to describe such experiences, but even more difficult would be to pretend one is above such things—trauma, a complex, the condition of being hunted. It was a reality deeper than any logical explanation that I tried to clarify for myself. At the same time all antisemitic remarks fueled this reality of fear, stress, and complexes.

At the end of 1958, the Białokamiński couple left Poland for Israel and they settled in Gedera, south of Tel Aviv. They were the last and only cousins of mine who survived the war and had stayed in Poland. Białokamiński was the son of Grandfather Mechel's sister. He had spent the war years in Russia, which explains his survival. At the beginning of the war he met Uncle Majorek somewhere in the east and brought us the only news we received about him.

The Białokamińskis were the only true support for me. They had supported me so many times psychologically, morally, and materially. Accepting their heartfelt invitation, I spent the last weeks before Tomasz's birth and the first weeks afterward in their home in Sosnowiec and they had helped us in the purchase of, and the move to, the cottage in Rejmontów. Białokamiński was a noble-hearted, upright, and decent man. He treated Rafał with respect and kindness. He loved Tomasz and always asked after him. After their departure I had no family at all left in Poland. I felt their absence, but still, there was Rafał and little Tomasz.

There was also Heniek: Though far away in Paris, he remained very close to me through our contact via letters. In Paris, Heniek had also started from scratch and the first years were very difficult for him; he could barely make ends meet, especially since he had hooked up with crooked partners, who wasted the fruits of several years of his labor. Later, he began faring better and on July 12, 1959, he married Rosa Wiener. Rosa had survived the occupation in a labor camp and after the war emigrated to the US, together with her mother. Several years later, she returned to Europe and there she met Heniek.

Heniek, knowing full well the poverty prevailing in Poland, helped by sending parcels with food and clothing, as well as money. It obviously seems natural that he remembered me, but he also remembered all those who helped us survive, above all Aunt Miecia and Tola. For many years, until his death, he helped these two women by sending them money every month. After Heniek's death, Rosa continued his show of gratitude—and does so to this day.

A confluence of several circumstances made us feel constricted in Rejmontów, so we started looking for a new apartment. We kept thinking about Poznań or Warsaw, but a lack of offers for an apartment exchange and our limited financial resources made such plans unfeasible. Rafał finalized the sale of his property in Rychwał and with the sum of money at his disposal we bought a house in Swarzędz, near Poznań. We moved there in the middle of 1962, in time for Tomasz to start attending first grade of elementary school. The

(Heniek) Henry Landschaft with his wife, Rosa, c. 1961

purchase of a new house turned out to be a misfortune. We had been deceived: The house was not finished, which explained the low price. We thought that we would manage to finish the renovations so that we could finally settle into a new house. Rafał was pleased with the large garden. However, we did not know that the house had been built on wet soil, which had neither been professionally drained, nor prepared for construction. We were flooded constantly, the basement was covered with water, and moisture crept up all the walls and rooms. Renovations lasted forever. Tomasz was getting sick again and had to be under medical care all the time. He was sent to the sanatorium in Rymanów Zdrój. Doctors recommended changing living quarters. I was completely exhausted. Everything seemed to conspire against us.

Once again—this time we promised ourselves it would be the last time—we started looking for a new place to live. I admired Rafał, who was 70 by that time, for managing to summon so much energy and goodwill to move once again. Most of the chores associated with buying a house—checking offers, consultations, and other formalities—fell on me. However, I was determined to find a new place for us, a new house, this time the last one…

We moved to Anin, a small locality within the bounds of greater Warsaw. After our experiences in Łódź and Swarzędz, I was obsessed with the issue of dampness. The first thing I looked for during various negotiations was the soil substratum or rather whether there were pine trees growing there, as a guarantee of dry ground.

In Anin, we purchased a semi-detached cottage, whose construction was not yet completed. The inside was unfinished and the external walls were not yet plastered, but despite the lack of central heating, the house was dry and warm, and we immediately felt better. Our mood also improved because of the proximity to Aunt Miecia, Maryla, and Hania.

Once we settled in Anin, Rafał resumed contact with Władek Kłoszewski, who lived in Warsaw. Rafał's former student from before the war, and our friend from the period under occupation in Opatowiec, was very attached to Rafał and had great respect for him. It turned out that the Warsaw archbishop, Bronisław Dąbrowski, had also been Rafał's student at the Królikowo elementary school in Grodziec. Kłoszewski had kept in touch with the archbishop and told him that Rafał Kałowski lived near Warsaw and about Rafał's war experiences. Archbishop Dąbrowski expressed his desire to meet his former teacher and invited him to his residence. Rafał willingly accepted the invitation and was very pleased with the meeting.

Rafał with Sabina Kałowski and his friend and former student Władek Kłoszewski, 1969 (left)

In the successive postwar years, I was troubled by the need to start searching for my mother's grave. She had died in 1929 in Kraków when I was barely four years old and was buried in one of the Jewish cemeteries in the city.

Before the war, Grandmother traveled every year to her daughter's grave. She didn't take me with her, but always promised she would take me with her when I was older. As a result, I didn't know where my mother's grave was or even whether the cemetery had survived the war. However, my vicissitudes after the war prevented me from embarking on the search for the grave and it was only after we settled in Anin, and my son was several years old, that I could return to the issue of my search. Together with Tola, I traveled to Kraków, where we went to the Jewish community office. A brief search through the archives turned up documents about my mother's death and information on the location of the grave in the cemetery on Miodowa Street. I was given a schematic drawing of the location. It seemed that everything would be quite easy.

We set out immediately for the cemetery. However, when I saw the condition of the place, I was overcome with doubts as to whether we could find my mother's grave. We went to the right, then to the left, and slowly got lost among the graves with barely visible Hebrew inscriptions, overturned tombstones, and paths overgrown with weeds. The cemetery seemed drowned in the thicket of grass, weeds, bushes, and trees. There was no way we could orient ourselves in the topography of the cemetery in accordance with the drawing. Tired, resigned, and helpless, we decided to give up. On our way out, we met an older woman who was busy cleaning some graves and watering the flowers, and I told her about my problem and my helplessness in trying to find my mother's grave. She showed interest in my search and promised to help. I left her with information about my mother and the schematic drawing of the location. Her name was Luna Halkowska, a resident of Kraków whose loved ones and friends had been buried in this cemetery. Six months later, Mrs. Halkowska contacted me with good news: Together with her son Henryk, she had managed to locate the grave. It was one of those accidental meetings, providence, when meeting with a stranger bears fruit.

I returned to Kraków, met with Mrs. Halkowska, and together we went to the cemetery. After more than 30 years, history had come full circle—through prayer and thoughts by my mother's grave—and brought me back to the years of early childhood, from which a blurry face of my mother emerged, the memory of her voice, and the warmth of her hand. It seemed terribly distant—before the nightmare of the Holocaust and all the troubles that befell me during the successive decades.

The grave was in a state of neglect, but the tombstone was in place. With the help of Mrs. Halkowska, who knew local craftsmen, I restored the grave, repainted the inscribed letters, and ordered a horizontal plaque to be put on the grave, on which inscriptions in Polish commemorated my mother and other members of the Landschaft and Chęciński families murdered during the war by the Nazis. At the bottom I placed the names of myself, Heniek, and Tomasz.

For years afterwards, until she died, Mrs. Halkowska cared for the grave at my request. I visited the grave many times since it was not only my mother's resting place, but also a symbolic grave of my family, who had been murdered in various places and concentration camps.

On one occasion in 1964, I traveled to visit Tola by train. Opposite me were two ladies and I heard them talking about Opatowiec. I introduced myself, saying that during the war I had lived in Opatowiec for many months. One of them turned out to be Janek Pociej's wife. She was a lawyer and was returning from a trial in Kraków. She wasn't from Opatówiec, and had married Janek only after the war, but she must have known the history of the town during the occupation from the stories of her husband. We began reminiscing about various events.

"Oh, now I know," she suddenly said. "My husband courted you. But don't worry," she added with a smile, "I won't scalp you."

We continued talking about the war years and how Opatowiec remained close to our hearts. This is how fate adds new events in the mosaic of history.

FROM POLAND TO DENMARK

The year 1968 came. At Heniek's invitation, I traveled with Tomek to France and we spent one summer month there. In Poland, the anti-semitic mood was growing in severity. We, too, found it difficult to go on, especially psychologically and spiritually. The decision to leave Poland was slowly maturing. But where should we go?

In Heniek's view, we should have gone immediately to Israel. I spoke to my acquaintances about possible directions of emigration, even though there were not many with whom we could talk about those matters. People spoke about Denmark and Sweden, where many Polish Jews emigrated after March 1968. I learned that it would be relatively easy to go to Denmark, a country that took in Jewish émigrés without any preconditions. In contrast, emigrating to Sweden necessitated fulfilling certain requirements such as level of education, professional specialization, etc.

We lived from day to day facing material difficulties. I was no longer working, and Rafał received only a small teacher's pension. Heniek helped us, of course. Without his help, it would have been very difficult for us to make ends meet.

Finally, we decided to emigrate. In June 1969, Tomasz completed elementary school and passed his entrance exams to high school. For six years we had tried to renovate our home in Anin, but the exterior of the house had remained unplastered, so selling the house wasn't so simple. At that time, no one from outside Warsaw could be registered as a city resident, which meant that we couldn't sell the house to anyone outside Warsaw and the offers that came from within Warsaw were unacceptable. In the end, constrained as we were by external circumstances, we sold the house for below the market price. When the buyers learned that we were selling the house because of emigration, they deliberately took advantage of the situation, and lowered their offer accordingly.

Rafał decided to stay. At 75 he thought he was too old to move and begin again. He helped us as well as he could in our preparations, but at the same time he was torn by the prospect of tearing the family apart. All he wanted was a room for himself in Warsaw. I argued against it. He had always lived in his own apartment and now he was supposed to live in a corner somewhere? Thus, in a great hurry I had to solve another problem: finding and purchasing a small apartment for Rafał. I found such an apartment on Saska Kępa, and after the transaction was completed and other formalities attended to, Rafał moved in.

Before the departure I had to attend to some unpleasant formalities, including "renunciation" of my Polish citizenship and handing over my identity document. In actual fact, we were stripped of Polish citizenship, but the communist rulers perfidiously portrayed this act as "voluntary" renouncement. In various offices I was treated impolitely, brusquely; many times, people showed me their animosity and I was treated with contempt, as someone who was being done a favor, while showing me their superiority.

I spent the vacation months of 1969—July and August—feverishly coping with the formalities and preparations for emigration. The entire situation weighed heavily on my heart and left me embittered. The date of departure was set by administrative powers and I was supposed to leave with Tomasz in August, but then he experienced health problems, which remained half-diagnosed. A series of tests followed by therapy was required and I notified the security office that I could not leave at the appointed date because of my son's illness, but they didn't want to reschedule the date of departure and prolong my stay in Poland. I kept going to the government office in an effort to explain the reasons for the delay of my departure. The officials treated me with arrogance, threatening me, "Either you leave, or you don't. We can cancel everything!"

I had with me a certificate from the district clinic about my son's illness and the ongoing series of complicated tests. I showed them the certificate, saying, "My child is ill. He is undergoing a series of complicated tests. I cannot leave with a sick child." Condescendingly, they changed the date of our departure to the beginning of September.

As émigrés, we could leave Poland with our furniture and household utensils—all within the limits set by the Polish authorities. We didn't take advantage of this "magnanimity," however, for objective reasons: There wasn't anybody who could arrange the transport. I was extremely busy with the formalities and was also psychologically devastated by the prospect of parting from Rafał and Poland. Tomek was still a child, while Rafał was still caught up in the dilemma of whether to leave with us or stay in Poland.

Just prior to our emigration Tola arrived in Warsaw from Jędrzejów, and stayed with us for two weeks, helping Rafał with moving out, as well as packing, preparing custom clearance, and many other small chores which kept mounting. For example, we had to draw up a precise and detailed list of the contents of our suitcases. At the customs office in Warsaw, officials concluded that Tomek and I constituted an incomplete family, therefore we could only take with us a smaller amount of necessities.

Aunt Miecia, who had been living in Warsaw for quite some time, also came to help us with the packing and simply to be with us, cheering us up in those difficult moments. I wasn't able to pack myself because of fatigue, stress, the bitterness of departure, and the sorrow of parting from the people close to me.

Ultimately, we hardly took anything with us. We had only two suitcases, with basic personal necessities, two sets of bed sheets, and a few books. Aunt Miecia wailed, "God help you, Dzidka, you are leaving without a single plate or pot."

"If I live, I'll have more than that," I replied.

I left with Tomek on September 8, by train from Warsaw to West Berlin. At that time, it was possible to get a sum of money for transportation costs through the Dutch embassy, which represented Israel's interests in the country. There was a special fund for this purpose, and the émigrés did not have to pay travel costs, which were exorbitant for Polish nationals. Officially, we were leaving for Israel, but because I knew that we were going to Denmark, I didn't want the fund to pay for me, and I bought the tickets with my own money.

Tomasz and I departed without being part of any emigration group. All I had with me was the address of the police commissariat in Copenhagen, where I was supposed to report immediately after our arrival. We were traveling without any money. In the case of emigrants, possibly even those who were not Jewish, the Polish authorities did not allow even the customary sum of five dollars given to tourists going west. I had money, but in order to avoid possible complications I left all of it with Rafał, as I was afraid to take even a small amount of money "illegally" out of the country. I was completely exhausted by the departure itself and all the preparations, and did not want to create new stress, problems or trouble. As a result, we didn't have a single dollar with us. I found 20 zlotys in my handbag, which somehow escaped inspection, but outside Poland they were worth nothing. At the Polish–German border the departing Jews were checked very thoroughly by the border officials, who conducted thorough customs checks and searches. Fortunately, we were not subjected to these humiliating "formalities." However, when the train was already in East Germany, a German conductor came in and, after inspecting our tickets, requested an additional payment. I told her I didn't have any money and after an unpleasant conversation, she left empty-handed.

Tired from the difficult journey and the entire preceding period, we fell asleep. The train stopped in East Berlin and we continued to sleep. I woke up when the train was already being shunted and when it stopped again, we jumped out in a hurry. Nervous and half-conscious, we grabbed our suitcases and my handbag, but because of all the commotion, I forgot to take the bag of food and drinks and we were left without any provisions.

In East Berlin we transferred to another train, which headed north to some Baltic port city in East Germany. The entire train moved onto a ferry and in this fashion we arrived in Copenhagen. We were tired, hungry, and thirsty, and I had not a penny on me.

We found ourselves in Denmark as stateless persons, without a passport or nationality. With just two suitcases, we found ourselves in a new, strange country, not knowing anyone, and without any knowledge of the strange language. We were exhausted from the journey, the stress of the preceding period, and by the parting from the people close to us.

Once again, the world in which I lived—Poland—closed its gates after me. I left Poland not through free choice, but as a result of being pushed to make that decision through several circumstances. What kind of choice was it supposed to be when we left under the pressure of coercion? Poland, with so many chapters of my life, remained behind a curtain, and for me, an iron curtain. At that stage, in 1969, I thought that returning would be impossible. Rafał and I parted with our hearts torn, each of us harboring doubts as to whether we were doing the right and good thing. Despite the physical distance, we still kept on considering the pros and cons of every situation, every decision that aimed at our departure and final parting.

Time seemed to stop at the train station in Copenhagen. What now? Where to? Towards what? It was September 9, 1969. We left the suitcases in the locker at the station. Payment was required only when you picked it up and we set out for the city. We kept losing our way, blundering through the alleys of Copenhagen, asking passersby for directions to the police commissariat, whose address was the only point of contact we had. The city pulsed with movement and the din of voices. Shop windows attracted our attention with their gay colors and variety of merchandise. We passed street stands filled with fruit and flowers. We were getting tired, hungry, and thirsty, but we couldn't afford to buy anything.

Finally, we reached the police commissariat, where we were greeted warmly and politely. We presented our documents—the certificate of identity, and the tickets confirming our travel from Poland to Denmark. The commandant asked us, "Where is your luggage?"

"In the train station locker," I replied in German.

"And why don't you have it with you?" he asked.

"Because we walked here from the train station," I said.

"What do you mean?" asked the policeman in astonishment. "You should have taken a taxi."

"Taxi?" I replied. "It was impossible. We don't have a penny. We were not allowed to take foreign currency out of Poland."

Of course we could have hailed a taxi from the train station to the commissariat and then asked the policemen to pay the fare. However, I didn't want to present them with a *fait accompli,* so to speak, without having any knowledge of how we would be received and treated.

Everyone in the commissariat was extremely polite to us. Right away they took us back to the train station in a police car, where they paid for the locker, and then together we returned to the commissariat. The policemen drew up an official protocol of our arrival in Denmark, gave us a sum of money for the most urgent purchases, and then escorted us to the harbor where a permanently docked ship functioned as a temporary hostel for émigrés.

Once aboard the ship, we met with representatives of the Danish organization Dansk Flygtningehjælp (DRC, the Danish Refugee Council), which deals with emigrants and refugees from all over the world. They cared for us with great solicitude. We were allocated a cabin and ate a free breakfast on the ship. Once a week we were given a sum of money for food and petty expenses. The DRC also took care of clothing, medical care, and help with translations. All the officials and social workers with whom we met were truly very warm toward us, full of goodwill to help us in every way—something completely different from Poland.

While we were living on the ship, a team of journalists from a Danish radio station came with a translator to interview Tomasz. He told them about ideological indoctrination in schools, teaching children untruths, while falsifying history and contemporary events. This was especially felt in civics classes, as well as in Polish language and history. He explained how students were told to denounce the State of Israel and the Zionist movement in accordance with official propaganda. Needless to say, most students either had no idea or didn't care about these subjects. Tomasz, who was brought up by Rafał in the spirit of knowledge based on truth and honesty, was aware that the school youth were being lied to, subjected to party ideology, and brought up in the spirit of intolerance. In the words of a 15-year-old, he recounted his experiences which had already become part of his biography, and darkened the contours of his youthful optimism.

We lived on the ship for six weeks, and then the DRC rented a room for us in a hotel, where we stayed for the next six months. During that time, after the initial period of acclimatization and getting used to our new living conditions, we began attending a Danish language class. After completing the month-long basic course, Tomasz was placed in a Danish boarding school, located not far from Copenhagen. Subsequently, the DRC allocated us a small apartment. We got it as an exception, without any effort, perhaps because there were only two of us—mother and son. The Danish were so dedicated to helping the refugees that they even apologized, saying that perhaps the apartment was not what I would have wished for. But I didn't have many requirements; I didn't come to Denmark for a more comfortable life.

Immediately upon our arrival I wrote a letter to Rafał, recounting our journey, the beginning of our life in Denmark, and gave him our address. He replied immediately, and we continued to write letters to each other on a regular basis. He was missing us. Before our departure he reassured us, keeping his best face, that he would take care of himself, that he had family and friends. In fact, he was alone: He had no relatives in Warsaw; Poznań was not close by and in any event, due to the harsh conditions, he could not travel in winter. He would visit his relatives in Poznań or Rychwał for a day or two, only to return to his empty Warsaw apartment. He kept deliberating what he should do. However, the longing for his wife and son turned out to be stronger than all his limitations and weaknesses, including those of age. Rafał decided to come to Denmark to see us and find out if he would be able to stay in the country for good.

On the basis of my formal invitation, Rafał arrived in Denmark in February 1970, only a few months after our parting. He arrived on a tourist visa valid for three months. At that time, I was still living with Tomasz in the hotel while the apartment allocated to us was undergoing renovation. Meanwhile, I rented a room for him in the same hotel and finally, we were together again.

During Rafał's sojourn in Denmark, Heniek organized for the three of us to visit Israel. From Copenhagen we flew to Frankfurt, where we met up with Heniek and his wife, Rosa, and then all of us flew to Israel. For the three of us, it was our first trip to the Land of Israel. Rafał traveled unofficially because, from the point of view of Polish law, such a visit was illegal. His Israeli visa was issued by the Israeli embassy on a separate form, without entering it into his Polish passport. We stayed in Tel Aviv for a month, during Passover and Easter, and visited Jerusalem and other sites. We also went to visit some distant relatives who had survived the war. We returned to Denmark in April and shortly after that Tomasz and I moved into the renovated apartment, whereas Rafał returned to Poland.

Rafał was very pleased with his visit to Denmark and the trip to Israel. He saw for himself how we lived, the living conditions in Denmark, his son's education. Earlier, he had had fears that, on account of his age, he would be a burden on me in a completely new situation and that it would complicate my first steps in my new life. However, he saw for himself that things were different and that he could come to the country and receive a permanent visa—as part of the reunification of families without any difficulties or objections. He returned to Poland with the intention of immigrating to Denmark.

Immediately after his return to Warsaw, he began preparations for coming to Denmark for good. He had to attend to many formalities, which kept multiplying as he went from one office to another. He sold the apartment on Saska Kępa and after seven or eight months, at the end of 1970, he arrived back in Copenhagen. We lived together for the next seven years, until Rafał's death in the fall of 1977.

Considering his age, Rafał did quite well. Instead of taking a course in Danish, he learned the new and difficult language at home. He perused textbooks, prepared grammar tables, and studied pronunciation. He watched Danish TV, wrote down new words, classified them, and studied various books on Danish conversation for foreigners. He devoted a lot of time to learning the new language and started to speak it.

About two months after our reunification, Rafał went through a crisis of sorts. His female cousin, at whose address he had registered himself, wrote a letter to him, saying that she was continually receiving all kinds of official letters, queries whether he intended to return to Poland, and summonses to sort out his pension issues, which meant that the authorities wanted to stop paying him his pension. Here, in Denmark, where he had come to stay for good, Rafał had to submit a formal application for asylum status. His request was granted without delay, but when the letter from his cousin arrived, his old dilemmas and wavering returned once again. He was faced with the prospect of severing all administrative and official ties with Poland, thereby closing the door on his past. He felt he was being deprived of a sense of security, which stemmed from the formal guarantee of being able to return to his native country. He kept asking himself and me, "What have I done? Now I won't be able to return."

I tried to reassure him. The anxiety he carried all the time within himself, and which was now resurfacing as a result of his cousin's letter, stemmed also from his awareness that his life was drawing to a close. He wanted to be buried in Poland, something which he mentioned to me on several occasions. He was very vexed by these questions, but in the end he calmed down. True, he missed his native country, and the garden we had in Anin and for which he cared greatly. At the same time, however, he was glad to be with us, that all of us were together, and he felt safe with his family.

In Poland, he had always been in opposition to the ruling system and communist power. He was upset by the limitations on public and political life, and the prevailing atmosphere of lies. He listened all the time to Radio Free Europe, made notes, liked to engage in discussions about politics, and was not afraid to present his critical opinion of the Polish political system. But when he settled in Denmark, he missed Poland and felt separated from the country.

Meanwhile, Tomasz graduated from high school and enrolled in the University of Copenhagen to study psychology and after two years of studies he went to Israel for six months. On returning to Denmark, he did not resume his psychology studies, but enrolled in the architecture department. He received his degree only after the death of his father.

In 1973, the three of us traveled to Italy. Rafał, who was then over 80 years old, was very pleased. This trip, and especially touring Rome with its history and works of art, as well as the Italian landscape, turned out to be one of our few shared experiences which were pervaded by a sense of peace, easiness, and inner calm.

The years in Denmark kept flying by, and I felt more and more at home. Gradually and to some extent, I managed to shed the fears and complexes that I had been carrying with me and which I had brought to Denmark. Only in Denmark could I look at things from a certain distance and realize that, due to the many circumstances and various conditions, I had lived in Poland as if constrained by a corset, without ever fully being myself, if at all.

After arriving in Denmark, I felt a certain inner relaxation vis-à-vis my last period in Poland, which unfolded in the shadow of antisemitic propaganda, anti-Jewish incidents, anti-Zionist campaigns in the street, in the media, and at school, and then coping with the decision to leave my native country.

In Denmark, I found no trace of the atmosphere that had surrounded me in Poland, none of the aggressive shouting which kept resonating in my ears, none of the inscriptions which remained in my memory for a long time: "Jews out!"; "Down with the Jews!"; "Jews to Israel!" and so forth. There was no anti-Jewish propaganda at all in Denmark. The Danes were very open, kind, without a shadow of animosity or acting superior towards us and other refugees and strangers. After the March 1968 events in Poland, the Danes took in Polish Jews without any preconditions, limitations or prejudices. They granted asylum and helped in every way. We were helped by state institutions, social organizations, volunteers, and ordinary people—neighbors, teachers, etc. To this day, after 30 years of life in Denmark, I have never experienced any unpleasantness on account of my origins and ethnicity. I have never experienced anything but good in my adopted homeland.

In Denmark I resumed working for a while, but then all kinds of maladies and illnesses started to afflict me—life was presenting me with its bill. I was hospitalized on numerous occasions and there, too, I was cared for with great

Rafał & Sabina Kałowski, Rome, 1973

dedication, never being told that I was an outsider or a stranger. Due to my impaired health, I was given an invalid's pension and Rafał, too, received a Danish pension.

On the wave of the March emigration of Polish Jews, about 2,500 people arrived in Denmark within a relatively short time. This was a lot for such a small country to absorb. In fact, the Danes were not prepared to take in such a large group of refugees, but they also thought that such circumstances could not be an excuse for refusing asylum. They made up for all insufficiencies and inconveniences by their kindness, willingness to help, dedication, and sacrifices. I was deeply moved and even embarrassed when they apologized for my discomfort, or tried to explain certain shortcomings.

The kindness showed to us, Jewish refugees from Poland, by the Danes were rooted in their attitude towards the Nazi extermination of Jews in World War II. Their attitude to Jews during that period was exceptional and diametrically opposed to the inferno of "the Final Solution of the Jewish question," and deeply empathetic to the bitterness we felt when returning to our homes, searching for relatives, and starting life anew after emerging from the hell of extermination.

The courageous response of the Danish king, Christian X, during the Second World War was well known—when, after overrunning Denmark, the Germans demanded that the Jews wear yellow armbands, the king was the first to oppose it, saying that the Jews were citizens of his country as much as any others. The Danes saved many Jews then by transferring them to Sweden. When the refugees returned home after the war, they found their apartments untouched, with all their furniture, household utensils, and even curtains on windows intact. They were watched over and taken care of by their neighbors, who openly and warmly welcomed back the returnees. How different, incredibly different, was this conduct from Heniek's and my experiences after returning to Jędrzejów, not to mention many other Polish Jews who survived the Holocaust and returned to their homes.

The attitude displayed by the Danes—a simple, everyday kindness—created a wholly different atmosphere, filled with cheerfulness and security. In Denmark, I discovered the normality of everyday life, beginning with stores filled with merchandise and the absence of waiting in lines, as well as through human kindness in even the most banal situations, and a sense of deep, inner peace. In Denmark, in the autumn of my life, I began to discover that the world could be different, both the world around me and the world within me. I managed to leave behind the fear that was part of me. Although, if truth be told, not quite: Only in Israel did I feel completely relaxed within, unwound, and peaceful at heart.

Rafał, who felt more and more at home in Denmark as the years passed, experienced all kinds of health problems, mostly due to age. His health required my great care and attention. Together we went to visit doctors and he was hospitalized on several occasions. Everywhere he was treated with kindness and respect and was examined and cured with great patience.

In the last period of his life, Rafał kept saying that he wasn't going to live forever and that he didn't want to die in Denmark. He kept returning to Poland in his thoughts and to the idea of returning to his homeland to die. He started going to the Polish embassy in Copenhagen to find out about possibilities of returning to Poland. He was treated brusquely, with a condescending smile and institutional cynicism, sometimes even with open brazenness. He was told to complete applications and explain the reason for his desire to return to the country. He was stonewalled, replies to his queries were delayed, he was told to wait or was summoned to the embassy for no reason, only to be told to come back on a different date. Put off on many occasions and humiliated time and again, he still pursued his quest to find a way back to Poland. He renewed his applications, but to no effect.

In February 1977, Rafał had a heart attack. Tomek, who was at home with his father at the time, kept his composure, immediately summoned an ambulance, and went with Rafał to the hospital. My husband stayed in the hospital for three weeks, and later had to take very strong medicine.

We saw how he tormented himself, how he was perfidiously treated by the functionaries of the communist diplomatic apparatus of the Polish People's Republic. Being aware of how adversely this situation affected him, I tried to dissuade him from persisting in his efforts. Time and again I explained that his trips to the embassy were for nothing, that they deliberately dismissed him and laughed at him. However, my laments were all in vain—Rafał was pigheaded and this matter became a sort of obsession for him.

One day, as he was leaving the embassy empty-handed as usual, he fell on the street. An ambulance took him to the hospital and I was immediately notified. I was petrified, but fortunately, he was able to leave the hospital after several days.

Tomasz, then 23, decided to go himself to the embassy and lodge a robust protest against the treatment extended by Polish officialdom to his elderly father. Before he left, Rafał asked him to be polite. Needless to say, they tried to treat Tomasz just as they had treated his father. However, he reacted decisively and determinedly, threatening them with intervention on a higher level. This seemed to have an effect: Rafał's appeal moved forward and, before long, he received permission to travel to Poland.

This seemed to have a calming effect on Rafał; the thought of the possibility of returning to his native country gave him a sense of security, and proved beneficial psychologically and spiritually. Later, he stopped talking about returning, and eventually didn't even want to return. But still, he felt completely different as the feeling of fear and being hemmed in left him.

However, illness, mostly circulatory, kept recurring. After his heart attack in February, Rafał was seriously weakened and in September 1977 he was hospitalized again. I visited him and often kept watch over him at night. Tomasz, too, devoted a great deal of time to his sick father—visiting him at the hospital and watching over him. During this difficult period, my friend Asia Klaper helped me a lot, accompanying me often on my hospital visits. Rafał grew weaker and he passed away in St. Joseph Hospital in Copenhagen, on October 9, 1977, at the age of 85.

Sabina & Rafal Kałowski with Sabina's dear friend Asia Klaper (left), at Strandboulvarden, Copenhagen (where they lived), 1977. Rafal passed away about three weeks after this photo was taken.

In conformity with his will I decided that he should be buried in Poland and, together with Tomasz, I attended to all the necessary formalities. It goes without saying that at the Polish embassy we encountered obstacles, difficulties, an absence of goodwill, and an unwillingness to help. How could we have expected otherwise? We had to secure a permit for transporting the body, permits for transport visas to Poland, and airline tickets. I attended to these chores in the shadow of my husband's death—the man who had rescued me during the Holocaust and then, together with me, had gone through all the difficult periods in our lives.

Rafał's body was embalmed, placed in a special metal container, and then, in accordance with Danish custom, put in a white coffin, which was sealed by an embassy official. The coffin was shipped by air to Warsaw and from there by car to Rychwał. Tomasz and I traveled by train from Copenhagen to Poznań, and then by car with Rafał's relatives to Rychwał.

We arrived in Poland for the first time since our emigration seven years earlier in order to bury a husband and father. Rafał's funeral took place in Rychwał, one week after his death, on Sunday, October 16. The body of my husband was laid in the Kałowski family tomb, which Rafał had built for his mother before the war. Immediately after the funeral I returned with Tomasz to Copenhagen. Another chapter of my life closed.

RETURNS: POLAND—ISRAEL—DENMARK

I returned to Denmark with Tomasz immediately after the funeral and he resumed his studies. For the umpteenth time history unveiled its paradoxical face. It had been Rafał who persistently and strenuously, facing obstacles that were placed in his path by the Polish embassy in Copenhagen, tried to secure consent for a permit to return to his homeland, but died in Denmark. I, on the other hand, returned to Poland after seven years to bury my husband in his family grave in Rychwał; this trip opened the psychological gates to my country of birth.

I returned to Poland again in 1979. I traveled to Kraków to visit my mother's grave, Tola in Jędrzejów, Aunt Miecia in Warsaw, Rafał's grave in Rychwał, and his family in Poznań. I crossed the length and breadth of the country, visiting the living and the dead. I was traveling into the depth of my history, which remained inscribed in Poland, into the depths of my childhood at my mother's grave, the depths of the tragedy of the *Shoah* in Jędrzejów, the depths of my postwar life decisions and the years spent with Rafał. Returning to Poland after not having lived there for ten years, returning from a distance of geography and time, once again renewed the question of the meaning of this history, the question of who I was. The thoughts and questions, which I thought had fizzled out a long time before, covered by the years, once again returned.

I could not free myself from this complexity of existence and identity. Once again, I relived the sorrow and the suffering of the events, experiences, and trials I had undergone in Poland. Why, I kept asking myself, while living there, did I have to flee all the time, to hide the person I really was, to not be myself? I wasn't and I am not, I thought, better or worse than the next person. I am the same human being as others. Why then, through all these years, despite the changing circumstances, did I hide my true self? This inner sadness kept on smoldering.

During my visit to Aunt Miecia, I went over with her the details of her visit to Denmark at my invitation, and from there her trip to the Holy Land, at Heniek's invitation. It goes without saying that the second part of this trip had to be carried out without the knowledge of the Polish authorities, because such a visit was illegal in light of Polish law at that time.

In accordance with our plan, Aunt Miecia arrived at my place in Denmark in 1979, and from there we traveled to Israel. At the Israeli embassy in Copenhagen Aunt Miecia was issued a visa on a special form, so that her passport would not bear an Israeli stamp. We spent three weeks in Israel, staying at a hotel in Tel Aviv, and from there we traveled to various places that Aunt Miecia, a devout Catholic, wanted to see. We visited Jerusalem, Bethlehem, Nazareth, and many sites in the Galilee, and around the Sea of Galilee. Aunt Miecia was deeply moved, and kept saying, "I couldn't even dream about ever being here." She was grateful to Heniek, who covered all the costs of our shared journey.

She always remained a person of noble uprightness, even at delicate moments. One day we were sitting on the balcony—Aunt Miecia, Heniek, and I—when during a conversation Heniek kept stressing how much Aunt Miecia had done for us in the years of the occupation out of her kind heartedness

Tomasz, Martin and Maryla Kałowski, 2012

and selflessness. Hearing this, Aunt Miecia was miffed and said, "Of course, but in truth I didn't do much. You owe your survival first of all to Rafał." We returned from Israel to Denmark, and later Aunt Miecia returned alone to Warsaw. Her Danish–Israeli journey lasted two months.

In 1980 and 1981, I followed from a distance the newly aroused hopes and dramas of Poland, through the fortunes of my dear ones and acquaintances. I sent food parcels to Rafał's family, especially to his niece, as well as to Tola and Aunt Miecia.

In 1984, Tomasz immigrated to Israel with his wife, Maryla. I considered following him there, but ultimately chose to remain alone in Denmark. It was too difficult for me to start life once again. I knew the country, but not as a resident, and not as one who could speak the language. Why would I want to be a burden on Tomasz? He went his own way, beginning—also not for the first time—a life in a new dimension, with his own family. In Denmark I had my own beaten paths, a circle of acquaintances, and habits.

I was left with the loneliness and anxiety for the children every time something dangerous happened in Israel. Loneliness and anxiety—my lifelong companions since my earliest years. There were also happy occasions, above all when, in February 1990, my grandson Martin was born. Now, all four of us could meet again, in Denmark or in Israel. I kept returning to Poland—to Tola, Aunt Miecia, Maryla, and Hania, and to the graves of Rafał and my mother.

Throughout all these years—the last ones in Poland, the years with Rafał in Denmark, then only with Tomek, and later being alone—the thought kept returning about writing this memoir, writing down—above all for myself—this strange story of life, rescue, and beginning anew several times, the story whose drama had always been close to my heart. This story had implanted itself so deeply that I couldn't uproot it—this life of escape, a kind of psychological flutter.

In my dreams I was faced with situations with no way out—I was on a moving train, I saw Germans, their uniforms, and felt the fear of being entrapped. I would wake up frightened, aching, and feeling suffocated. After so many years, these dreams still return once or twice a year. They evoke once again the situation of being trapped, with the same dark feeling of fear, which remains unbridled by the passing of time.

Doctors and psychologists explain that these traumas are so deeply embedded in my deepest memories that they will remain there forever, unable to be erased. It amounts to a kind of disability, afflicting those who have gone through the hell of "the Final Solution to the Jewish question." My experiences affected my psyche. After the war, when it seemed that everything was over—even though it was never over for me—the consequences of my past began manifesting themselves. I sought medical care many times to try to deal with the nerves, dreams, nightmares, and the desire to escape through the window when I dreamed about the Germans. At the same time, however, I was overcome by the desire to write and describe my personal history. As if by externalizing it—perhaps in expectation of lessening my pain—it would stop gnawing at me from within. Rafał and I discussed this topic many times, but I never made a practical step in this direction. There was never enough time, determination or propitious circumstances. Life kept bringing on new events, mostly difficult ones, which sidelined the intention to write. This was also the case after Rafał's death, and then, later, after Tomasz's departure.

On April 21, 1996, Heniek passed away in Tel Aviv. His illness had been long and difficult and his death affected me profoundly. He had been a pillar to lean on throughout my life and was my closest blood relation. Heniek had been faithful to his family year after year and we had been close and dear to each other through our shared war experiences.

On each anniversary of Heniek's death, according to the Jewish calendar, we gather for the memorial ceremony (*askara*) at his grave in a Tel

Aviv cemetery. In attendance are his wife, Rosa, myself (his niece), Tomasz, Maryla, little Martin, and a handful of relatives and acquaintances. A rabbi leads the prayers and ensures at least ten men are present to constitute a prayer quorum (*minyan*) so that the public prayers can take place.

In the last years of his life Heniek lived for a project, which he funded himself, to build a surgical ward in the well-known Ichilov Hospital in Tel Aviv. The construction continued after his death with the help of his wife, Rosa. The inauguration of the ward, Heniek's gift, took place on April 11, 1999, three years after his death. The ceremony brought together Heniek's loved ones and acquaintances, representatives from the Tel Aviv Municipality, health services, and social organizations. A memorial plaque was unveiled, commemorating the benefactors—Henryk and Rosa Landschaft—of this precious gift.

I began writing my memoir in the spring of 1997—the story that is mine and about me, but at the same time, also transcends me. I went to Poland again in the summer of 1997, but this time with the intention of visiting both new and old places, and the places where I had hidden 55 years before.

In Chlewice, I could barely recognize the old village. The building where the Grzegorek couple had lived was no longer there; the only house remaining was that of the Nowaks. I didn't find anyone there who remembered me from the war years. However, in the nearby village of Jarnowic I found Mrs. Pawlikowa, at whose place I had lived for a spell during the war. She was an old woman by then, but she remembered me, was very glad to see me, and recalled from memory many episodes from my sojourn at her house. In Włoszczowa I located Witek Nowak, who had had an engagement ring made for me more than half a century before. I visited Władek Felis, an employee on the Leszczyński estate during the war, who had been living for many years in Prząsław, near Jędrzejów. I had seen him 30 years before, several years before my emigration to Denmark. After the war Heniek and I gave him a gift: about two acres from the remains of my grandfather's field.

Finally, I arrived in Opatowiec, which I had left in March 1945. There I met Janek Pociej, a retired engineer. In Opatowiec it seemed that nothing had changed. The town, with its market square, church, and steep cliffs over the Vistula River, had become even more provincial, submerged in lethargy and provincial hopelessness. But the dock was no longer there, nor was the coal silo, and there was no movement on the river—the same river where I once spotted Heniek returning from the prison in Kraków. Instead of a small boat, there was a ferry attached to a rope, and the Dunajec River's confluence with the Vistula had been rerouted slightly. The remains of Mrs. Wawrzykowska's house were being gradually dismantled. Several hundred meters from there was a cemetery with the mass grave of the victims of the Opatowiec massacre carried out by the Germans, as well as the graves of others I used to know. In the distance was the forest to which we used to escape. Most of the houses in the market square and side alleys had remained intact.

Once again, I was in Opatowiec—the site of my history—and with Janek Pociej, a witness and also historian of the town. Together we recalled the events in which we had taken part. Each of us knew about different things, or remembered them differently, and our conversations turned into a mosaic of those dramatic days. Later, we corresponded with each other.

I returned to Opatowiec and Jędrzejów once again in the summer of 1998. The occasion for the visit was the death and funeral of Aunt Miecia Leszczyńska, who had lived in Warsaw until the ripe old age of 93. Before her death, she had known about my preparations to write this memoir and

(from left) Sabina, Tomasz (behind), Martin and Maryla Kałowski at the Yad Vashem ceremony honoring Rafał Kałowski as a Righteous Among the Nations, January 31, 2002.

encouraged me to persist in my efforts. Dear noble soul, Aunt Miecia. She was a mother to me and I was like her daughter, and she didn't hesitate to risk her life for me and her loved ones. I remember her from many events in the darkness of my tragic history, including the time when, moving from place to place, I had hidden in her house, and during the night she had come to caress me and tuck me into bed.

I kept fleeing from my story, but also kept running towards it. I relived anew the same pain, despair, and fear. I kept searching for events, faces, objects, glances, words, colors, and smells, which had been lost as the years passed by. With great difficulty, which cannot be put into words, I returned to the events that had taken place, but would not pass away and continued to exist. Even though my experiences of the Holocaust were more and more disdistant, at the same time there was a constant burnt offering, carrying its weight in my heart. Slowly, day by day, I carried this strange resistance of memory, but I was also being pushed by an irresistible power of will. I submerged myself once again into the known and yet strange reality. Reconciling myself with it, and yet never quite succeeding.

April 1999

ACKNOWLEDGMENTS

My life could not have been saved without the exceptional contribution and help, as well as love, sacrifice, nobility, and loyalty, of many people.

My thanks go to my dear grandparents and my father, who, in situations of mortal danger, transcended themselves by looking for a way to assure my survival, believing that it could be possible.

To Rafał Kałowski, husband and loyal life companion, to whom I owe my life above all.

To Mieczysława Leszczyńska and her daughters, Maryla, Hania, and Tosia.

To Tola Grzywnowicz.

To Władek Kłoszewski, the Grzegoreks, the Wieczoreks, and many others who, unaware of my origins, took part in my rescue.

To all, but in particular, Samy Baldiers, Paulina Damas, Beata Klaper, and Lusia Berkowitz, who were my spiritual companions in the years of working on my memoirs and this book. Thank you for encouraging me, coaxing me to continue the work that had already begun, and which so many times seemed to me an effort that surmounted my vital resources, psychological immunity, and spiritual strength.

To my son, Tomasz, who listened to and read these memoirs, made comments, and sometimes criticized in good faith. To my daughter-in-law, who also came to know these memoirs gingerly and patiently, and passed on to my grandson, Martin, fragments of my story. My beloved Martinek, who, at barely five, excitedly and expressively related the events of his grandmother's life to his kindergarten class in Tel Aviv.

To Mr. Ryszard, with whom we "revealed" to the world this volume of memoirs and who entered the story of my life with great feeling and personal engagement, exhibiting astonishing empathy and an understanding of events, feelings, and thoughts—so difficult to pass on—of someone who lived through the inferno of the Holocaust.

I thank you all through these memoirs... Shalom.

Sabina Rachel Kałowska